4-
2001

CLAUSEWITZ

on

STRATEGY

CLAUSEWITZ

on

STRATEGY

Inspiration and Insight from a Master Strategist

Edited and with commentary by
Tiha von Ghyczy, Bolko von Oetinger,
and Christopher Bassford

A publication of The Strategy Institute
of The Boston Consulting Group

JOHN WILEY & SONS, INC.

New York · Chichester · Weinheim · Brisbane · Singapore · Toronto

This publication is designed to provide accurate and authoritative information in regard to the subject matter covered. It is sold with the understanding that the publisher is not engaged in rendering professional services. If professional advice or other expert assistance is required, the services of a competent professional person should be sought.

Translated by William Skinner and
Peritus Precision Translations, Inc.

Maps on pp. 106–107 and 118–119
by Eureka Cartography, Berkeley, California

Photo credit: p. 14 courtesy of the headquarters
of the German army forces command, Koblenz

Library of Congress Cataloging-in-Publication Data

Clausewitz, Carl von, 1780–1831.
[Vom Kriege. English. Selection.]
Clausewitz on strategy : inspiration and insight from a master strategist / edited with commentary by Tiha von Ghyczy, Bolko von Oetinger, and Christopher Bassford; translated by William Skinner.
p.   cm.
Translation from German.
Includes index.
ISBN 0-471-41513-8 (cloth : alk. paper)
1. Military art and science.   2. Strategy.   I. Ghyczy, Tiha von.   II. Oetinger, Bolko von.   III. Bassford, Christopher.

U102.C6557 2001
355.4—dc21   2001017641

Printed in the United States of America.

10 9 8 7 6 5 4 3 2 1

Contents

The Strategy Institute of
The Boston Consulting Group

When Bruce Henderson founded The Boston Consulting Group in 1963, strategy in the business domain was largely unexplored. Although the basic principles of strategy had been well established in the military arena, and extended to the geopolitical realm, the concept—and the language—of competitive advantage had yet to be formulated. We at BCG are proud of our role in its initial development in the early 1960s and its progress since then. In an effort to continue pushing the boundaries of strategy, we have formed The Strategy Institute under the direction of Bolko von Oetinger.

The Strategy Institute investigates the nature of strategy. It is our belief that strategy is a combination of bold moves and flawless execution. In seeking the strategic insights that inspire bold moves, the Institute ranges far afield, often exploring ideas gleaned from disciplines far removed from business. The Institute frequently collaborates with leading academics and professional societies, working cooperatively to cross-fertilize strategic thinking. The interaction fosters a healthy symbiosis between businesss and academia—and among divergent academic disciplines.

The Strategy Institute intends to share its research with the public through articles and books. This is our first book. We intend to share many further insights over the coming years, with the hope that they will serve both to extend and refine the concept of strategy in business and society.

Carl W. Stern
President and Chief Executive Officer
The Boston Consulting Group, Inc.
January 2001

Acknowledgments

The editors would like to thank the many people who contributed to this book. Special thanks go to Nicholas Dew for his contributions in the early stages of our work and to Ted Buswick, whose unflagging dedication to this effort has been a source of energy to all of us. Ted and Matthew Wikswo gave us exceptional support and contributed greatly to the final shape of the book. Heidi Eckert provided outstanding administrative abilities, consistently kept us focused, and facilitated our often difficult communications across countries and states.

In addition, we thank Karen Hansen and Larry Alexander at Wiley for their belief in and support of our project, and William Skinner, Dagmar Dolatschko, and Peritus Precision Translations, Inc., for our new translation of Clausewitz that is so faithful to the original.

Many BCG professionals gave us thoughtful comments and encouragement, and the Darden School of Business at the University of Virginia gave one of us the opportunity to work on this endeavor. A special acknowledgment goes to BCG's Mark Blaxill, who got us started in earnest when he observed, "Clausewitz is cool."

Tiha von Ghyczy
Bolko von Oetinger
Christopher Bassford
January 2001

Prelude

Midnight, December 27, 1812.
Tauroggen, Lithuania.

The Russian army is pursuing Napoleon's rear guard as the French army beats a disastrous retreat back from Moscow. The Russians are camped for the night; the ground is frozen; snow is falling; visibility is low. The Prussian rear guard of the French army—conscripted to Napoleon's service after the defeat of the Prussian king at the battles of Jena and Auerstadt in 1806—lies less than a mile away.

Wrapped against the elements, an unarmed officer in Russian uniform leaves his tent in the Russian camp. Accompanied by a cossack, he exchanges a word with a sentry, passes through the line, and disappears into the night.

Thirty minutes later, he approaches an enemy outpost. Prussian hussars stop him and demand his business; in turn he demands to see the Prussian commander, General Hans Yorck von Wartenburg. Surprised at his perfect German, the Prussian sentries comply, and the general quickly discovers the agent to be no Russian at all.

Rather, he is a Prussian, just like the officers to whom he now speaks. They have remained in the Prussian army and serve their French conquerors under orders from their king; he has resigned the commission of the Prussian king in order to serve with the Russians and resist the Napoleonic machine. His purpose: to persuade his compatriots to defect from Napoleon's army—and thus to compel his king to join the anti-French alliance. The penalty for this bold stroke, if he is unsuccessful, will be death for treason.

Yorck weighs his options and wavers. Who is this out-of-place Prussian? Can he be trusted? Are his references to an impending massive Russian offensive credible? The shadowy officer returns to the Russian camp; the scene is repeated the following night. Yorck remains doubtful; he asks the Prussian to pledge his honor for the terms of the offer, and in response is told, "I pledge myself for the sincerity of this letter, upon the knowledge I have of General D'Au'vray and the other men of Wittgenstein's head-quarters; whether the dispositions he announces can be accomplished as he lays down, I certainly cannot pledge myself; for your Excellency knows that in war we must often fall short of the line we have drawn for ourselves."★ The officer withdraws again to the Russian camp. Yorck ponders anew.

The next morning, a handful of Prussian officers meet at a windmill near Tauroggen. Half are in the service of the tzar, half in the service of Napoleon. They conclude a treaty, declare the Prussian forces neutral, and inform their distant king. Ultimately, the king approves: Prussia breaks with France. Napoleon is doomed. The secret agent's gambit has succeeded.

That secret agent is Carl von Clausewitz.

★Carl von Clausewitz, *The Campaign of 1812 in Russia,* trans. Francis Egerton, Third Lord Ellesmere (London: J. Murray, 1843; reprint, New York: Da Capo Press, 1995).

INTRODUCTION

*In which the editors shun no effort to make the case
for why and how
this book must be read for greatest profit.
The author of the original work is introduced as
an outstanding thinker
who has shown admirable fortitude
in not letting his love for theory get the better of his keen sense
for practice.
The case is made that when all is said and done
strategy is no more nor less than
the search for new avenues of the intellect.*

There is scarcely a time that appears more foolishly chosen for theorizing than a period of intensive transition and instability. Yet such are the present economic times and such was the political environment that led Prussian philosopher of war Carl von Clausewitz (1780–1831) to expound his fundamental ideas on strategy. Many, like Clausewitz, seek clear order in thinking in and about an environment that seethes with disorder. They must be either satisfied with ephemeral fame, followed shortly by well-deserved ridicule after the first major event that contradicts the theory, or—to avoid this unpalatable fate—their theories must somehow penetrate to the very nature of instability itself.

On War (1832), Clausewitz's magnum opus, has never been in danger of derision or oblivion. It deserves, now more than ever, the full attention of the modern business strategist for accomplishing the unlikely feat of offering new ways to order thinking in disorderly times and provide steadiness in charting strategy in an unstable environment.

Carl von Clausewitz as a man is as worthy of consideration as the work itself. His values and intrinsic beliefs, more than his specific ideas, have given his work an inner coherence and a power of persuasion that have endured until modern days. These qualities are amply reflected in the work, and in what he thought and felt about events and people who were professionally or personally close to him. He may rightly be seen as an inspiration to all those whose ambition is to excel professionally in any field. It was his refusal, above everything else, to let his mind be constrained to a narrow point of view that must strike the modern professional as exemplary. Finally, he was a man of passion who knew joy and defeat in his private and professional life and allowed both success and defeat to mold his views.

THE SPRINGS OF INSTABILITY

The storming of the Bastille was as inessential to the underlying reality of the French Revolution as modern technology is peripheral to the no less revolutionary transformations in today's economy. The living reality of a revolution is never the sum of visible novelties but a central idea that resonates with many by virtue of its promise of liberation from constraints on the potential of individuals. For an idea to resonate widely and strongly enough to unleash the energy and imagination of many, it must have qualities that are achieved only in those rare historical instances when the aspirations of individuals crystallize around a common good and the means of achieving that good is within humanity's grasp.

The transformation of the economic and business landscape that we presently witness may yet suffer many reversals of fortune; it may slow down, find its way obstructed, and deviate into directions that no one can foresee, but the underlying idea has been gathering momentum and resonance since well before the advent of the Internet or even computers. It has grown into a great and irrepressible idea.

The idea is simply the notion of individuals, alone or in small groups, being able to determine and defend their economic autonomy. It is almost ironic that, in Marxist terms, one could speak of a vast redistribution of the means of production and the latest phase in dismantling the original state of economic affairs that led to Marxist thinking in the first place. To the chagrin, possibly, of some unrepentant Marxists, it is the economy itself and not class warfare that proves to be the most effective answer to their criticism. This redistribution we are now witnessing could not occur without new technology, but technology is not the stuff that dreams are made of. Dreams are always about freedoms.

In business there is general agreement that we live in a time of transformation akin to a phase transition in matter—all bets are off and all properties and rules are suspended until further notice. At the root of this conviction is the more or less explicit acknowledgment that there is indeed a revolutionary idea out there that has captured people's imaginations. It is not primarily technology that drives this transformation and makes it unpredictable, but individuals who seek to redefine economic relationships with the possibilities that new technologies offer.

This transformation will not be completed in a few years; it is more likely to last decades, during which we will see a perpetual turmoil of emerging technologies, business models, and even novel conceptualizations of national economies. We will see traditional economic agents and institutions disintegrate and new ones appear as if in some magic cauldron.

In such times, reliance on experience alone will be self-inflicted obsolescence, management tools will acquire a blunted edge as soon as they are conceived, and how-to prescriptions will hold the anti-quated charm of folklore at best. Yet the true building blocks for successful strategies will be more abundant than ever: passionate entrepreneurs, bold ideas and inventions, talented people, and the ability of imaginative execution liberated from many traditional constraints. These times will offer an embarrassment of riches for the true strategist.

It is the true strategist, who welcomes rather than fears such times, who can benefit most from the work of Carl von Clausewitz because *On War* is quintessentially a philosophy of strategy that con-tains the conceptual seeds for its constant rejuvenation. It is a phi-losophy that fuses logical analysis, historical understanding, psychological insight, and sociological comprehension into an encompassing exposition of strategic thought and behavior. It is a philosophy that effectively prevents strategy from ever degenerating into dogma. It is a notion of strategy for revolutionary times.

BUSINESS IS NOT WAR

Business is not war. The occasional statement to the contrary, made to emphasize the heat of the battle in business competition, is tolerable journalistic hyperbole. Business and war may have many elements in common, but as total phenomena they will remain separated forever by the distinct and irreconcilable nature of the forces that give rise to them and the outcomes they engender.

It is impossible to conceive of business without value creation for the benefit of society or without the desire of individuals to be productively engaged in society. Today, this is truer than ever. Traditionally dominated by large organizations, business has become the primary stage for the creativity of citizens seeking economic independence and the thrill of the marketplace. There is none of this in war.

We caution the reader against the temptation of seeking to rigidly map war onto business and vice versa. Such mappings can be and have been done at the cost of gross distortions and with no other benefit than some semantic entertainment and a few very forgettable platitudes. The distortions arise because there are elements of business (such as the customer) and elements of war (such as annihilation of the enemy) that simply do not have their equivalents in the other realm.

Yet, don't we—in presenting this version of *On War* to the business audience—encourage the very temptation that we exhort the reader to resist?

In exploring Clausewitz's selected and rearranged thoughts as presented here, we hope to let the reader abstract from both war and business and encounter at that level of abstraction something that is not only mappable but, in fact, common to both: strategy.

AFFINITY OF STRATEGIC TIMES AND MINDS

As perplexing as this may appear at first for a work on warfare, Clausewitz speaks loudly and clearly to the modern business executive who is inclined to listen. He does not, of course, speak the language of today's audience. He does better: He speaks the executive's mind. This affinity of minds is so palpable that it would not have been hard to translate the Clausewitzian language of war into the language of contemporary business, but such a crude undertaking would be unworthy of reader and author alike.

How can a military work from nineteenth-century Prussia speak our strategic minds undiminished and unmuted by the passage of time, the vastness of societal transformation in nearly two centuries, and the stark differences between war and business? Because—in essence—Clausewitz saw, experienced, as well as reflected and acted on the same basic realities that we face today. He can speak the executive's mind because it is his own.

But hold it a moment! Let us envision the modern business leader who is in charge of a successful organization in this economic transition with its new technologies, global capital markets, deregulation, the Web, takeovers, mergers, entrepreneurial challenges, cyber money, and other turbulent phenomena that herald massive and surprising changes. None of these realities are present in military affairs and certainly not in nineteenth-century Europe, whose image appears to us colored by romantic images, gentle manners, and courtly glamour.

Yet under that surface of gallantry, refinement, and romantic effusion, the reality of Europe was of massive and unprecedented turmoil brought about by the clash between the vigorously emerging young Prussia in conflict with a mighty France rendered unstable and unpredictable in the throes of its internal transformations; by alliances made, broken, and reconstituted at dizzying speed; and by the rapidly arising concept of a nation-state commanding economic and human resources on a scale never witnessed before. Napoleon's Grande Armée was more than 450,000 men strong as it marched on Russia. Although France's population growth has been slow (from 26 million in 1800 to 60 million today), that force would be equivalent in our time to about 1 million armed men crossing several thousands of miles. This was (and still is) stunning. To recruit, arm, train, feed, and move such a gigantic army, entirely novel methods, technologies, and organizations had to be and were created. (Instrumental to the French campaign of 1812 in Russia was the invention of canning food by the French confectioner Nicholas Appert in 1810.) There had been many conflicts and wars before but never undertaken with comparable determination, ingenuity, and complete disregard for the traditional rules of the game. Turbulent, chaotic change—then and now.

Engaging Clausewitz

Struck down by cholera at the age of 51, in the prime of life and at a time of renewed ascendancy in his career, Clausewitz was well short of completing the work to which he had dedicated most of his intellectual energies.

It was left to his wife, Marie Countess von Brühl, whose romantically happy life with Clausewitz was well known in Prussian society and who was his unlikely but more than capable intellectual companion in his inquiries into the nature of war, to undertake the posthumous publication of his disorganized manuscripts. The book appeared in 1832 under the title *On War* (*Vom Kriege*).

The book became an instant classic and has been acknowledged ever since as one of the canonical books of Western culture. Often quoted yet seldom read, its reputation is based more on legend than on an actual assessment of its profound merits. It has repeatedly been decried and demonized as a celebration of unrestrained violence by critics who mistook Clausewitz's sober discourse on war as endorsement of its horrors and failed to realize that almost all thinkers of this age (Kant and Rousseau were major exceptions) considered war, rather than peace, the normal state of affairs. *On War* has also been criticized—less unjustly—as excessively philosophical, paradoxical, inconclusive, and altogether impenetrable.

There is no shortage of quotations from *On War.* It has been suggested that no other work has been quoted by so many who have not read the source. Although the isolated statements most often quoted

Love in the Life of Clausewitz

In 1831, Clausewitz was stationed in Poland, where he was observing an anti-Russian rebellion and organizing a sanitary cordon to contain an outbreak of cholera. He wrote to his wife frequently, and a letter of July 29, 1831, contains a remarkable premonition of death and an anticipation of his final farewell:

> Today word came that the Russian army has begun moving against Warsaw. If so, then the last great decision will soon come to pass, one that I look forward to anxiously. If I should die, dear Marie, that is simply how things are in my profession. Do not grieve too much for a life that had little left to undertake in any event. The foolishness is getting out of hand, no one can fight it any more than one can fight cholera. At the very least, dying from the former entails less suffering than dying from the latter. I cannot say how great is my contempt for human judgment in leaving this world. This disease is sure to run rampant, and I would not have survived it at any rate; so little is lost.
>
> What causes me deep sorrow is that I did not take greater care of you—it was not my fault. I thank you, dear angel, for the help you have given me in life.

> When I first beheld you, I felt
> As though in the presence of an angel's majesty,
> I trembled through and through
> And my heart whispered a childlike prayer:
> Stay, kind stranger, stay here in this world below,
> Through your eyes' beautiful gaze, bless and
> Lead me back to life's tranquil peace
> From all the storms of life!
> You gave me your hand in friendship,
> Under an angel's protective wing.

Our path winds gently through life,
And in heaven resides our bliss.

Do you recognize these lines? They were there at the outset
of our alliance, and should be there at the end, as well. I embrace
you, dear angel, until we meet again in better circumstances.

Carl von Clausewitz   Marie von Clausewitz

do have a startling and arresting quality (who is not familiar with
"war is merely a continuation of policy by other means"?), the indis-
criminate use of quotations has done more to obscure Clausewitz
than the 170 years since his death. The quotations—far more than
the widely unread work itself—have contributed to the popular misconception of Clausewitz as a cold and callous prophet of total,
unconditional war. The real logic of Clausewitz—unquoted and
indeed unquotable—has remained buried for all but the few who
have struggled with the original. Yet it is precisely Clausewitz's train
of logic that merits the full attention of those interested in strategic
thinking and practice.

On War's fearful and infamous reputation with the public never
appears to have deterred the most capable and daring minds of the

military, social, political, and economic sciences from returning to
the wellspring of insights that it contains.

With this present edition, the recently established Strategy Institute of The Boston Consulting Group wishes to offer that same
opportunity to the modern business reader: to explore the riches of
Clausewitzian thinking that we consider to be universally applicable
to strategy. We thought that this book should be relatively brief but
challenging, capable of steeling the mind for strategic discipline yet
expanding the mind's appreciation of new opportunities. Yet the
encyclopedic scope of *On War* is simply too vast for ready access,
and its purely strategic essence is easily missed behind the work's
specific concern with military matters.

Thus we have taken enormous liberties with *On War*, excising
what is not broadly strategic and rearranging the flow of the text to
emphasize the coherence of Clausewitz's arguments. We have not,
however, altered the text itself, nor modernized the nineteenth-

---

The Hardships and Rewards of Reading Clausewitz

If the following review, taken from a military journal of 1832, is anything
to judge by, it seems that *On War* has never been an easy read—even in its
own time and language. But secondary accounts cannot reveal the full
measure of Clausewitz's rich and nuanced thinking, and readers who wish
to take advantage of his full value have no choice but to wrestle with him
in his own words. Fortunately, as the author of this review also realized,
the potential rewards for that effort are great.

> But this spring whose crystalline waters stream over particles of
> pure gold does not run in a flat riverbed accessible to all; rather,
> it flows in a narrow, rock-bound valley surrounded by gigantic
> ideas, at the entrances to which the great mind stands guard like
> the cherubim with their swords, turning back anyone seeking
> entry merely for the price of a fleeting intellectual pastime.

century tone. And we too have resisted the temptation, as we cautioned the reader to do likewise, to map the original military logic onto today's business reality because we feel that the act of doing so is our readers' prerogative and their own proper reward for the effort that lies ahead. We have added some additional commentary and relevant texts in sidebars placed throughout the book to further stimulate the reader's own journey. In exercising such caution and restraint we hope to have acted in the very spirit of Clausewitz whose predominant concerns were to make clear that, in strategy, there is no room for doctrinaire thinking and that theory serves the talented practitioners by expanding their powers of observation and sharpening their instinctive sense of judgment in action.

As a tribute to the personal relationship that Clausewitz considered paramount in his life, we have also included the original introduction to *On War* by his wife Marie Countess von Brühl. Her words not only expand our knowledge of Clausewitz's career, disappointments, and hopes, but also shed light on the romance, deep affection, and mutual respect that characterized the bond between them.

Although far less forbidding than the original, this book is still abstract and short on concrete advice. To those who seek the silver bullet in strategy, these characteristics will be liabilities. But to those who realize—as Clausewitz was the first to do—that without full freedom and sovereignty in execution there can be no strategy, these characteristics will be indispensable virtues. It is the respect for the executive's freedom in the exercise of the powers of mind that led Clausewitz and, in turn, us to retain a certain level of abstraction and to refrain from prescriptive advice.

The remainder of this introduction is organized in three parts. The first offers a historical sketch of the life and influence of Clausewitz. The second explores the workings of the mind engaged in the exercise of strategic thinking. The third part invites the reader to explore modern business realities through the optics of Clausewitzian thinking and to appreciate the views of a Prussian military theorist of land warfare in nineteenth-century Europe as stunningly commensurate with the realities of global business today—not for having anticipated our times or our business environment, but for having revealed the essence of strategic deliberation.

CLAUSEWITZ IN HISTORY

Of all the great books in the Western canon, only two address the fundamental problems of war. One is by the Athenian writer Thucydides: *The Peloponnesian War* (c. 400 B.C.). The other, *On War,* is widely acknowledged as the greatest of all the classical works of military theory. After more than a century and a half, Clausewitz continues to exercise a powerful influence on modern strategic analysts, theorists, and practitioners. His work remains the most comprehensive, perceptive, and modern contribution to political-military thought—and to the subject of strategy itself.

Clausewitz was a complicated man both of action and of thought, and he left a complicated legacy by no means easy to describe. The meaning and practical impact of his theories are subjects of hot debate, and the lessons taken from his works vary dramatically depending on the times, the circumstances, and the interpreter. To form any meaningful personal assessment of the value of his ideas, it is important to understand Clausewitz as a living personality. He was much more than a military academic. He was a practical soldier of wide experience, a historian and historical philosopher, and a political theorist. Personally sensitive, shy, and bookish by nature, he could also be passionate in his politics, in his longing for military glory, and in his love affair with his wife—with whom he built an intellectual partnership that draws modern attention for reasons having little to do with his military reputation. In combat, he regularly displayed coolness and physical courage. He was untouched by scandal in his personal life, and his intellectual integrity was remarkable; he was utterly ruthless in his examination of any idea, including his own. His keen analytical intelligence was accompanied, perhaps unavoidably, by a certain intellectual arrogance—the latter quality amply demonstrated by many sarcastic comments that appear in *On War.* His own personality and temperament were not of the sort he describes in his famous discussion of military genius and the ideal of the great commander. Rather, Clausewitz was essentially a brilliant subordinate of the type who helps his superior to better understand himself, his goals, and the obstacles to their achievement. And that is also the role of the body of theory he created.

Clausewitz was born on June 1, 1780, near Magdeburg in the kingdom of Prussia. He lived in a period of tremendous upheaval and turmoil, and therefore had the opportunity to observe sweeping changes in almost every aspect of political and military life. Under Frederick the Great (ruled from 1740 to 1786), the small Prussian state—essentially the family business of the Hohenzollern family—had through superb leadership and management transformed itself into one of the great powers of Europe. The era of the French Revolution (1789 to 1815), however, ushered in a new social, political, and military era in which Frederick's successors found it difficult to compete. Fortunately for us, Clausewitz had the wisdom, insight, and energy to recognize the meaning and implications of those changes, and to capture that recognition in ideas that remain relevant to us today, in a period of similarly revolutionary change.

He entered the Prussian army as a cadet at the age of 12 and first saw combat at 13 in a vicious war with revolutionary France. After Prussia withdrew temporarily from the Wars of the French Revolution in 1795, Clausewitz applied himself to his own education. Beyond strictly military subjects, he developed wide-ranging interests in art, science, and education.

All of these interests were to have an impact on his thinking about strategy. So successful were his efforts at self-education that in 1801 he gained admission to the Institute for Young Officers in Berlin, which would eventually evolve into Germany's famous

General War College. He quickly came to the attention of the new director (and future army chief of staff), Gerhard von Scharnhorst, a key figure in the Prussian state during the upheavals of the Napoleonic Wars. Clausewitz graduated first in his class in 1803 and was rewarded with the position of military adjutant to a young prince, bringing him into close contact with the royal family. Given the poverty and dubious nobility of Clausewitz's own family, this was quite an accomplishment, and it permitted him to fully exploit the cultural and intellectual resources available to the state's elite in Berlin. Thereafter, despite the political stresses of revolution, war, defeat, and eventual Prussian triumph, Clausewitz would remain near the center of political-military events and decision making in the Prussian state. However, his intellectual integrity and unflinching devotion to the preservation of Prussia's independence and

Colonel Clausewitz in 1815, seated at the table (left) with Baron vom Stein and General Gneisenau, key figures in Prussia's political and military resurgence.

power would occasionally make him unpopular with the nation's political leaders, who were often cowed by Napoleon's brilliant but fleeting successes and thought more in terms of short-term personal survival than of long-term strategic success.

Alarmed at devastating French victories over Austria and Russia in 1805, Prussia mobilized for war in 1806. Though confident in the legacy of Frederick the Great, the Prussian forces were shattered in humiliating defeats in battles at Jena and Auerstadt. In the peace settlement, Prussia lost half of its population and territory and became a French satellite. Defeat was both a shock and an eye-opener for Clausewitz. He recorded his impressions, both of the war and of the dismal sociopolitical condition of Prussia, in several short articles. In broad terms, Clausewitz's argument was that the French Revolution had achieved its astounding successes because it had tapped the energies of the French people. If the Prussian state were to survive, much less prosper, it had to do the same. This would require sweeping social and political reforms in the Prussian state and army. Clausewitz's works therefore reflect a strong impulse toward social and military reform. However, neither he nor his mentors desired a social or political revolution, only such changes as were necessary to preserve and expand Prussia's independence and power. When he returned in 1808 from a period as a prisoner of war in France, he joined energetically with Scharnhorst and other members of the reform movement, helping to restructure both Prussian society and the army in preparation for what he believed would be an inevitable new struggle with the French.

His enthusiasm was not, however, shared by the Prussian king, Frederick William III, who was more concerned with maintaining his position in the much-reduced Prussian state than with a nationalistic crusade. Clausewitz's disillusionment with this timid brand of leadership reached a peak when Prussia, allied with France, agreed to provide an army corps to Napoleon to assist in the 1812 invasion of Russia. Along with a small number of other officers, Clausewitz resigned from the Prussian service and accepted a commission in the Russian army. Clausewitz, the careful analyst and philosopher, thus staked his career, reputation, and very life on what was essentially a roll of the dice. It is perhaps not all that surprising, however, that he won the toss. He had argued as early as 1804 that Napoleon's system would not work in Russia.

In the Russian service, Clausewitz participated in the long Russian retreat in the face of the Napoleonic invasion of Russia, and then in turn witnessed the French army's own disastrous retreat from Moscow. Slipping through the French lines, he played a key role in negotiating the Convention of Tauroggen, which brought about the defection of General Yorck von Wartenburg's Prussian corps from the French army and eventually forced Prussia's hesitant leadership in the anti-French coalition.

None of this won Clausewitz any affection at court in Berlin, where he was referred to on at least one occasion as "Louse-witz." Still, Prussia's change of sides led, after some delay, to his reinstatement as a full colonel in the Prussian army. Clausewitz participated in many key events of the War of Liberation (1813 to 1814), but chance and the lingering resentment of the king prevented him from obtaining any significant command. He served instead as an aide to General Gneisenau, one of the principal leaders of Prussia's military rebirth. He sometimes found himself in the thick of combat, as at Lützen in 1813, where he led several cavalry charges and was wounded. During the Waterloo campaign in 1815, Clausewitz served as chief of staff to Prussia's 3rd Corps. Outnumbered 2 to 1, his force played a crucial role in preventing vital reinforcements from joining Napoleon at Waterloo.

In 1818, Clausewitz was promoted to general and became director of the General War College in Berlin. Because of the conservative reaction in Prussia after 1819, during which many of the liberal reforms of the war years were weakened or rescinded, this position offered him little opportunity to try out his educational theories or to influence national policy. He had little to do with actual instruction at the school. Clausewitz therefore spent his abundant leisure time quietly, writing studies of various campaigns and preparing the theoretical work that eventually became *On War.*

Clausewitz returned to active duty with the army in 1830, when he was appointed commander of a group of artillery brigades stationed in eastern Prussia. When sudden revolutions in Paris and Poland seemed to presage a new general European war, he was appointed chief of staff to Field Marshal Gneisenau and the only army Prussia was able to mobilize, which was sent to the Polish border. Although war was averted, Clausewitz remained in the east, organizing a sanitary cordon to stop the spread of a cholera epidemic from Poland. He and Gneisenau both died as victims of that epidemic in 1831.

Before he left home in 1830, Clausewitz had sealed his unfinished manuscripts. He never opened them again. Just what his book might have looked like, had he completed it to his own satisfaction, is an entertaining but usually fruitless subject of speculation for military scholars. In any case, it was Clausewitz's intention never to publish it in his own lifetime. That decision freed him of concerns that his own ego or career concerns would affect his style and conclusions, reflecting the unrelenting integrity of his approach to the complex subject he had chosen. As he had planned, his wife Marie—who was intimately familiar with his ideas and method—edited his unfinished manuscripts and published them as his collected works. The first three volumes—*On War*—appeared in 1832 and have had a profound impact on thinking about war, politics, and strategy ever since. *On War* has been translated into every major language and many minor ones.

As a result, Clausewitz's conceptions run like a subterranean river through all of modern military thought. We find them in the writings of the Marxist-Leninists and Mao Zedong as often as in those of recent European and American commanders, political scientists, and military historians.

Nonetheless, *On War*'s influence has historically risen and fallen inversely with the military fortunes of its readers, perhaps because of the widely noted difficulty of the book. Only a serious military reverse, it seems, can force ponderous governmental and military institutions to wrestle with the complex realities Clausewitz describes. The book's origins lie in Prussia's own devastating defeat by Napoleon in 1806, and it found popularity in Germany following the widespread revolutionary movements across Europe in 1848. In France, it first developed a serious audience following France's humiliation by Prussia in 1870 to 1871. In Britain, it drew a large audience immediately following the inglorious Boer War of 1899 to 1902.

Despite the intense interest of individuals like Dwight Eisenhower and George Patton, American military institutions became interested in *On War* only in the wake of the debacle in Vietnam. The subsequent resurgence of those institutions has clearly found its intellectual inspiration in Clausewitz. Clausewitzian arguments are prominent in the most authoritative American statements of the lessons of Vietnam and dominate the curricula of America's war colleges today.

In an exhibition of the 424 most influential books of the Western world that took place in London in 1963, *On War* was listed under the heading "The Philosophy of War," and Clausewitz joined the company of such authors as Augustine, Archimedes, Machiavelli, Newton, Rousseau, Kepler, Cervantes, Kant, Leibniz, Darwin, Goethe, Humboldt, Byron, Einstein, and Churchill. The British historian Stanley Morison commented: "These thousand pages occupy a unique position among military writings of any age and nation. The book is less a manual of strategy and tactics, although it incorporates the lessons learned from the French revolutionary and Napoleonic wars, than a general inquiry into the interdependence of politics and warfare and the principles governing either or both."★ Indeed, Clausewitz's unique historical contribu-

---

★John Carter and Percy Muir, *Printing and the Mind of Man* (London: Cassell & Company, 1967, p. 180).

tion consists of not following any formal military rule, but of approaching the phenomenon of war *philosophically*. And in the 1970s, historian Michael Howard pointed out that Clausewitz's "thinking today enjoys a degree of influence such as it has not possessed since the heyday of the Prussian General Staff in the latter years of the nineteenth century."★

Anyone interested in understanding the fundamentals of strategy in any field is thus well-advised—one is tempted to say obliged—to become familiar with the concepts of this most influential of military thinkers. Given the admitted difficulties, however, of digesting Clausewitz's massive and sometimes overpowering tome, most of us are forced to look for some more expeditious method of accessing his insights—hence the present volume.

CLAUSEWITZ IN THE MIND

There is something mildly irritating about most theories of human affairs.

In the study of nature, the methods of inquiry and the results derived with the help of theory convince and even please us. Yet the same theoretical approach applied to social and economic interactions leaves us wavering between high hopes of having found a key to resolving the complexities of life and foreboding that our hopes will turn out to be misplaced. At first we realize that with each insight gained in human affairs new and deeper questions present themselves, just as in the physical sciences. But then we realize that with each apparently firm insight into human reality we can act on the insight and thus alter the very reality we had hoped to understand, and this is very different from our interaction with the physical forces of nature.

★Michael Howard, foreword to *Clausewitz: A Biography,* by Roger Parkinson (New York: Stein & Day, 1979).

Nowhere is this more troubling than in the study of affairs relevant to leadership, which, by its very nature, must alter and not merely understand human realities. Such is the case with strategy.

Practice and Theory

The practitioner who studies conventional theories of strategy is almost certain to suspect that the author of any given theory has more or less deliberately disregarded an elementary feature of leadership in action: the fact that in all realms of human interaction institutions seek leaders precisely because they require people who are flexible enough not to rely on any fixed theory. Once this suspicion has taken root it is not easily dispelled, and theory will appear as unreliable sophistry. Indeed, if one truth can be obtained from previous and simpler truths by the straightforward application of logic—as conventional theory would have it—why do society and business put such a premium on imaginative leadership, which defies such logic and flouts precedent?

This polarity between what we expect from theory and what we know to be the primacy of practice in human affairs is what led Clausewitz to relegate theory to the proper yet modest role it may occupy, but never exceed, in the service of practice.

This act of restraint, reasoned modesty, and intellectual integrity is Clausewitz's strongest credential for being considered the deepest thinker about strategy. It is an act that no true strategist can fail to emulate.

Since the dawn of Western thought, the twin concepts of theory and practice have drifted apart and are now often regarded as polar opposites. Derived from the Greek words θεωρειν (*theorein*, to look at, contemplate, inspect) and πραττειν (*prattein*, to do, act), the concepts were once inseparable, as in the admonition "think before you act." Theory was the act of the eye surveying thoughtfully and—in this sound Hellenic sense—all sane humans were the-

orists inasmuch as they cared to use their powers of reasoning. Theory, understood as the act of the thoughtful eye, is precisely what
commanders and business executives must rely on when charting a
course amid the turmoil of events and uncertainties. And theory as
guidance for the thoughtful eye is what Clausewitz offers.

In our time it is not uncommon to see practitioners proudly
belittle theoretical accomplishments and theorists disdainfully ignore
sound practice. In a very real sense neither side can be blamed; their
attitudes are a reflection of how far theory and practice have drifted
apart. Both sides suffer the consequences.

Those practitioners who, confident in their accomplishments
and practical ability, deride contemplation, usually glorify energy,
dedication, skill, instinct, and innate talent—at least until circumstances or a cunning opponent fashions a trap that these virtues
alone, unaided by contemplation, will fail to detect. Success will
then indeed prove to be its own mortal enemy.

In contrast, those who put their faith in theory may not even
have the dubious pleasure of becoming the victims of their own
success. Their efforts may never go beyond elaborate plans that are
easily punctured by a forceful competitor.

On War can be read as a general road map for finding the way
out of this conundrum of theory versus practice. The path is steep
and narrow, however, and great strength of will is required to follow
it, for it leads through perplexing contradictions, while on either
side broad avenues beckon the weary traveler toward the comforts
of either theory or practice.

The steep and narrow path was the one Clausewitz took in his
relentless search for theory that is relevant to practice. In pursuing
it, he willingly risked alienating not only the theorists (by abandon-
ing the pursuit of categorical truths) but also the practitioners (by
constantly exposing the vulnerability of practical wisdom to unusual
circumstances brought about by chance or a creative opponent). For
Clausewitz, taking this path was a fearsome leap indeed, for as an

educator on military matters he must have been keenly aware of his students' desire to obtain the secret of success in a few easily memorized formulas.

Seldom, if ever, before or after Clausewitz has Western strategic thinking, military or otherwise, risen to such intellectual honesty and modesty in appraising what theory can and should be for those entrusted with decisions and execution.

Pole and Counterpole

Physicists can define light by reducing it to more basic constituents: waves or photons. In practical situations, however, a person of action may be better off thinking of light as the absence of darkness. To one intent on letting light penetrate the darkness, it is more useful to know what causes the shadows than to know what a photon is.

Such juxtapositions of opposites abound in human discourse and have been at the root of both Western and Eastern philosophies since antiquity. Commonly referred to as dualism in Eastern religious reflection and in pre-Socratic Greek philosophy, this type of thinking reappeared as transcendental dialectics in the works of Immanuel Kant and acquired a somewhat dubious reputation as a result of Hegel's subsequent historical dialectics, which, in turn, led to Marx's material dialectics.

Although clearly influenced by Kant, Clausewitz's use of opposites is most reminiscent of the Greek philosophers. The earliest institutions of Western education in Greece offered only two courses: rhetoric and dialectic. The former is the art of persuasion at public gatherings and the latter is the art of reasoning carried out in a learned dialogue between philosophers of opposed views. *Dialectics* was synonymous with *logic* from antiquity until relatively modern times. The *Oxford English Dictionary* defines the term as "the art of critical examination into the truth of an opinion; the investigation of truth by discussion." Unlike Hegel and his followers, who propose to resolve the opposites at a higher level, Clausewitz does not resolve the opposites. In his view, it is not the resolution that matters but the perennial altercation between opposing mental pictures of reality held in the mind of the commander.

The unresolved contradictions between such polar opposites may at first vex those whose natural inclination is to ask which of the poles is to be preferred. Is it attack or defense? Strategy or tactics? Surprise or consistency? Clausewitz's deft evasion of all such questions may test the patience of even the most philosophically inclined, but those who adopt the method as their own will soon find it revealing to view business situations dialectically.

Throughout his book, Clausewitz seems to delight in increasing the tension between the polarities and the overall tension of the work as layer after layer of polarities is added. True to his conviction about the realities of conflict, Clausewitz never wavers in withholding the resolution, and the book is one of suspended tension—very much like reality itself.

Will and Counterwill

Clausewitz's use of polarities and the dialectic method was not merely an exercise in deliberately unconventional thinking, a matter of whim, or a vainglorious attempt to appear different from his contemporaries. Rather, it was firmly grounded in sound reflection on the subject matter. Whether our interest is in games, contests, war, or business competition, the clash of opposing forces is a given. If these forces cease to be in opposition, there is nothing left to investigate.

The most fundamental element common to all strategy, and the root polarity in Clausewitz's thinking, is the clash of antagonistic, purposeful, and intelligent wills between opponents, be they enemies at war or businesses in competition. In most of our daily activities, we do not face the prospect of an intelligent and resourceful opponent intent on thwarting our plans. In the absence of such an opponent, the task ahead may still be formidable and require all our knowledge and luck, but it would merely muddle our analysis to call such situations strategic.

Having established the clash of opposing wills at the center of strategic thinking, Clausewitz can proceed to dismantle the false hopes of planning that so often creep into strategy. He shows that the uncertainty in all strategy is not an extraneous nuisance, but a necessary companion. Uncertainty in strategy is not merely an inability to forecast external events but—far more important—the consequence of the indeterminancy of events brought about by intelligent and resourceful opposition. Because his metaphors of friction and fog so clearly encapsulate the inevitability of uncertainty, they have become central concepts well beyond the military arts. True strategists must not lament uncertainty, but embrace it as the wellspring of their art.

Conflict and Opportunity

As polarities accumulate in the Clausewitzian edifice and resolution is withheld, one naturally starts to wonder how decisions should finally be arrived at. If neither defense nor attack is unequivocally good or bad in a given situation, if neither surprise nor perseverance can be firmly recommended under certain conditions, if it is not clear whether one should unite one's forces or split them, the normal course of decision making seems to be utterly compromised. Of what possible use or value can such a theory be?

It is comfortable to rely on prescriptive theories, and nowhere is this truer than in business. Although few of us believe in silver bullets, it is as hard to resist such theories as it is to refrain from formulating them. In Clausewitz, we encounter the most resolute denouncer of all such theories. His implacable opposition to and savage criticism of what he calls a *positive doctrine* deserves thoughtful consideration.

Prescriptive theories are so tempting because they often serve us exceedingly well. In taking a prescribed medicine, we rely implicitly on a prescriptive theory of medicine. We save money for retirement on the basis of prescriptive theories and implement logistical systems in the expectation that prescribed measures will yield the desired effects. But in none of these situations do we face an intelligent and resourceful opponent—none of these situations is strategic. This distinction is the crux of the matter and the boundary beyond which prescriptive theory should not venture. In strategy it is only a matter of time before all contestants, constantly seeking advantage, acquire the same set of silver bullets. Only for the briefest of moments can prescriptive theory transcend the equalizing forces of competition—the intelligent clash of wills.

That doesn't mean that prescriptive theories are entirely worthless. Clausewitz, in fact, assumes that his students will study military history and be well acquainted with what has worked in the past. Having a silver bullet is clearly a great deal better than not having it, but is simply not good enough to confer strategic advantage.

Instead of prescriptive theory, Clausewitz recommends thoughtful contemplation (in the original sense of the Greek "theory") that the successful general or business executive must continually practice. If thus engaged, the executive's mind constantly swings between conflicting viewpoints, allowing talent and experience to determine the exact position leading to action.

In the dynamics of execution, under the ever-changing conditions of the surroundings (whether terrain and weather in war, or the economy and consumer attitudes in business), the contestants must unceasingly evaluate the potential advantages to be gained from shifting their perceptions between any number of polar opposites. The resulting thought process can be seen as the trajectory of an irregular pendulum that swings in more than one plane.

The contrast between the Clausewitzian method and prescriptive theory, in which polarities are reconciled and tension is relieved, is sharp, and we are naturally drawn to the latter, which offers more certainty and fewer ambiguities. But consider the price one must pay later in exchange for comfort now. The theory that offers apparent truths will center the mind on those truths and force it into a small, constrained orbit around them. It will dull the mind's perception of subtle (and not so subtle) changes in the environment. In removing the pain of struggling with ambiguities, it blinds us to emerging opportunities that no conventional theory can ever fully anticipate. The cure is worse than the disease.

Method and Genius

What leaders, generals, or executives can reasonably be expected to act, and rely on large organizations to follow them trustingly, if their minds are tracking a multidimensional pendulum? Surely, they would have to be geniuses!

The notion of *genius* is central to the Clausewitzian view of the individual shaping strategy and execution. The contemporary connotation of genius may be more exalted and restrictive than the meaning attributed to the word by Clausewitz. To quote Clausewitz himself:

> *Each particular activity, if it is to be performed with a certain amount of virtuosity, requires specific aptitudes of the mind and heart. When these qualities are present to an exceptional degree and are demonstrated through extraordinary achievements, the term* genius *is used to describe the mind to which they belong.*
>
> *Of course, this word is used with a great variety of meanings, and for many of these meanings, defining the essence of genius is very difficult indeed. But since we do not claim to be experts in philosophy or language, we may be permitted to adhere to a meaning that is familiar to us from common usage, understanding the term* genius *to denote a greatly enhanced mental aptitude for certain activities.* ★

★This quotation can also be found at the beginning of the chapter, "The Coup d'Oeil."

Clausewitz leaves no doubt about how he wishes the term to be understood. He is not talking about the divinely inspired prodigy who appears as brightly and as infrequently as a comet. *Genius*, as he defines it, encompasses qualities we expect to find in thousands of people who are given positions of leadership in business and other realms of public life.

Yet, even in light of this more modest definition of genius, one must wonder of what possible use theory could be to those who possess genius, who can rely on instincts, mental aptitude, and innate talent. Is the Clausewitzian method offered to those who need it least, or not at all, or—even more disturbing—whose talents may suffer in the confinement of theory?

Although overpowering in its scope as well as in its depth of inquiry, Clausewitz's work is essentially a model of professional humility. Good theory should serve genius just as a superb trainer serves a modern athlete: No matter how much trainers may know and no matter how much influence they may have, their entire professional accomplishment must reside in laying the foundation for achievements they can never anticipate and in stepping back when the moment of competition arrives.

Principle and Imagination

Let us stray for a moment into the domain of chess—far simpler than business or war, but indisputably deeply strategic.

A novice chess player soon learns that it is a good idea to control the center of the board. This recognition will recur, in novel disguises, in situations far from the chessboard. It may help to seek the equivalent of the center of the board in any situation, or to see that the role of the center has migrated to the flanks, or to realize that there is no board and no singular topology. In most situations, applying the same recognition literally would be irrelevant at best.

In discovering the malleability of this and other principles—off and on the chessboard—our novice chess player will take the first steps toward mastery, which is not merely of principles, but over them. There will be maddening defeats—worth more than victories—where strict adherence to a principle will be the Achilles' heel that a more nimble opponent can exploit. Later still, when teaching novices, the former novice will not hesitate to declare the principles sacrosanct with a knowing but inward smile and the confidence that he has done his best to show them the road, but not travel it in their stead.

Bobby Fischer, the former world chess champion, whose brief but intense career illuminated the firmament of chess as it has seldom been before, boldly proposed that the rigid placement of pieces on the board at the start of the game be abolished in favor of a more random scheme. More specifically, he proposed that the pawns be placed as usual and the major pieces (king, queen, rooks, etc.) remain on their prescribed rows, but that their positions on that row be randomly scrambled.

Is this just another example of Fischer's supposedly bizarre behavior? We do not think so. The rigidly regimented opening position has, over the last two centuries, led to an elaborate theory of opening moves. The ambitious player either hunkers down to penetrate theory and thus forfeits months and years of valuable practice, or else adopts some tenets of the theory unquestioningly. The game itself and the community of players are worse off either way, because theory is no longer the search for malleable principles in dynamic succession, but a rigid edifice administered by a clergy of experts. Fischer's proposal is a call for revolution, a call to abolish the rigid edifice and send the high priests of opening theory back to the tournaments to show their mettle. At a deeper and more significant level, his proposal addresses the survival of the game itself. Oppressed by theory, the game is becoming increasingly less attractive to the young, and without youthful players there will be no game. Only unsurpassed mastery of, and love for, the game could have led Fischer to seek to restore the malleability of principles.

Fischer's proposal may never be adopted, but in business, fortunately, entrepreneurs and innovative firms routinely defend the malleability of principles. We have whole armies of Fischers to blast through principles if they begin to harden into dogma. It is the very hardening of minds that fuels the entrepreneurial challenge.

Viewed in this fashion—and this is the view adopted by Clausewitz, whose appreciation of talent was always greater than his respect for the rigid scientific concept of truth—principles are not only malleable, but more akin to the rungs of a ladder than to the foundational pillars to which they are more commonly compared. The best current principles are merely the most promising rungs leading to higher and better principles. But the rungs already mastered do not cease to matter completely. If they did, the edifice of principles would become as precariously unbalanced as a ladder whose rungs dissolved as one climbed higher.

If one thinks of the rungs of the ladder as principles and the entire ladder as imagination, one comes close to Clausewitz's underlying philosophy.

Execution and Reflection

Ever since Plato, humankind has been seeking to determine the qualities leaders must possess. What qualifies them to be raised above others, and what must they practice to sustain their legitimacy? We do not have a fully satisfactory answer, but perhaps it is the search that really matters.

Ever since Plato raised the question, his own answer—encapsulated in the notion of a philosopher-king—has been a source of inspiration and aspiration. Clausewitz's thinking is very similar and may be summarized in the notion of the scholar-executive. He demands that the general or executive remain a scholarly observer of reality as much as an active force. Nor is there any separation between the time for action and the time for scholarly reflection. They are one and the same: the here and now.

CLAUSEWITZ IN OUR TIMES

At the appropriate level of abstraction, war is merely an instance of strategy as it manifests itself. Chess and other games, sports, and business are other instances of the same manifestation. There is no doubt that studying strategy in the context of war can be a deeply insightful way of exploring business strategy as well. Business (unlike trade and commerce) is a modern phenomenon and nobody spoke of business strategy before the 1960s, whereas war is as old as humankind; the Chinese general Sun Tzu writing in the fourth century B.C. eloquently expressed central themes of strategy. Business is a latecomer to strategy and there is no strategic discipline comparable in seniority with war. Much can still be learned.

The Rise of Strategy

Significantly, the word *strategy* is a semantic latecomer and, unlike *tactics* that has preserved its meaning over time, was not used at all in its present meaning until shortly before Clausewitz embarked on his inquiry. A few words on its etymology may shed some light on the rise of the concept itself. A *strategus* was a military commander in ancient Athens and a member of the Council of War. This designation had its simple roots in στρατος (*stratos,* army) and αγειν (*agein,* to lead). Roman historians introduced the term *strategia* to refer to the territories under the control of a strategus and the word retained this narrow, geographic meaning until Count Guibert, a gifted French military thinker, who was deeply impressed and puzzled by the startlingly new quality of the campaigns conducted by Frederick the Great, introduced the term *la Stratégique* in the sense that we have adhered to since (*Défense du système de guerre moderne,* 1779). It is tempting to speculate that Frederick the Great's innovations in warfare formed the first coherent manifestation of strategy in practice that called out for a name of its own; that Guibert was the thinker to act on this semantic necessity to delineate tactics from something new and more encompassing; that Napoleon was the first to give the new word the fullest and ever since unsurpassed scope of meanings; and that Clausewitz was the first to go beyond the word and to illuminate the nature of strategy itself. Astoundingly, all of this happened in the span of less than 100 years between the first Frederician campaigns in 1740 and the publication of *On War* in 1832.

Continuing in a speculative vein, it is striking to observe that, in spite of the equally long histories of warfare and commerce, neither the military community before Guibert nor the business community before H. Igor Ansoff (*Corporate Strategy,* 1965) could see the strategic element in their domains clearly enough to give it a name. One is led to entertain the possibility that they were unable to see strategy in their fields not for want of vision but because of its absence, and that strategy cannot emerge until a system of human interactions reaches a certain critical degree of complexity.

The Adolescence of Business Strategy

The 30 or so years since business strategy has been conceptualized and practiced have been rich and exciting but cannot represent more than its infancy. It was a relatively sheltered infancy if one looks back with the benefit of some anticipation of what lies ahead. The pains and doubts, the thrills and joys of adolescence are just ahead of us in business strategy. Much as children enter adolescence and distance themselves from parental authority to seek out teachings that prepare for independence in thought and action, so must business strategy, on its way into adolescence, sever the comforting but restrictive ties to the authority that it relied on in the form of simple theories and ready-made tools. There is no more qualified source of teachings to accompany the adolescent business strategy (and strategists) than the body of thought developed by Clausewitz.

In that phase of transition between infancy and adolescence, parents lose their touch and fumble as awkwardly as their children grope around. Both discover that former tricks have lost their magic reliability. The theory and practice of business strategy is in similar straits. Things just don't work the way they were supposed to. Theory rushes breathlessly from one paradigm to the next leaving theorist and practitioner alike frustrated and exhausted. And in practice, we find the accustomed order of things is no longer valid. Customers act up and do things they were not supposed to; teamwork is often rather stale and hopelessly bogged down by compromise—a far cry from what it was supposed to yield; the value chain is breaking at places where no one ever suspected it to break. As exasperating as this may be in daily management, the transition itself, viewed from a greater altitude, is healthy and exciting.

Let us explore tentatively then how the mind-set that Clausewitz urges us to adopt would perceive some of today's business realities. This must be tentative, incomplete, and on a very general level in deference to the Clausewitzian imperative that such interpretation be left to the commander in the field and that under no circumstances should general reflection usurp the role of individual thinking and impede, rather than foster, the independence that adolescence calls for.

Uncertainty: Curse and Blessing

Uncertainty in the past (or at least in our recollection of it) is primarily associated with a few external events of an unpredictable and singular nature that suddenly intruded upon the affairs of a business or a country. International conflicts, revolutions, and acts of governments or gods were typical harbingers of uncertainty. These events were often singular, discrete, and sharply discontinuous. They agreed with our traditional notions of causality but they were nevertheless essentially unpredictable because the primary causes remained hidden until it was too late.

Uncertainty in our time has a markedly different quality. Phenomena seem to emerge without much advance notice but not quite as discontinuously as in the past, nor as a result of some fairly simple causal chain whose triggering mechanism is hidden. They "emerge" out of countless independent and minor human acts that gradually merge in a self-reinforcing tapestry of interdependence. The individual components are plainly visible although often impossible to enumerate.

Uncertainty in the past was mainly exogenous. It will be endogenous in the future. The primary sources of uncertainty reside now in how free economic agents rearrange the relationships among themselves in ways they choose. They are limited only by their imagination rather than, as in the past, by forces that economic agents had to obey. We can now say, paraphrasing G.B. Shaw: "We have seen uncertainty and it is us."

The notion of strategy without uncertainty is vacuous. Yet such a qualitative change in the nature of uncertainty must impact the nature of strategy.

As human as it may be to lament uncertainty, the time has come to abandon the view of it as an impediment to business and adopt the strategically sound view that this qualitatively new, postmodern uncertainty is the very engine of transformation and a constant source of new business opportunities. We cannot fairly complain about the (invisible) hand that feeds us.

Yet stopping the laments is not good enough. It also calls for a dose of Clausewitzian thinking. Business, compared with war, used to be glacially slow and disturbed only by singular events of external uncertainty. No longer. We think that it is reasonable to state that business has accelerated and has acquired the very dynamics that the fog of war and friction describe.

Rule Breaking as the Rule

Adherence to what is known to work serves imitation. Rules are the crutches that help imitators hobble along. Innovators also honor the rules, but in the breach. They may pay even more attention to the established rules but with a completely different intent: how best to get around them?

It may well be argued that business and the global economy are just now emerging from an almost medieval slumber. In the Middle Ages crown and church organized all aspects of life in an immutable hierarchy of supposedly divine origin, and this order gradually broke down as free cities started to flourish and interact with each other as they saw fit. A similar economic transformation is taking place now as the notion of free market capitalism spreads and traditional constraints on business activity are swept away on a global scale.

In the Middle Ages, the successful artist was celebrated for the faithful and technically brilliant execution of the rules of the art. The artist was a member of a tightly organized guild and essentially imitated the best in his own work and that of fellow guild members over and over again. Honoring the rules was a good idea if one cared about one's career, livelihood, and avoiding the stakes of the Holy Inquisition.

Since the advent of the Renaissance, artistic fame and fortune reside in honoring the rule in the breach. The guilds as enforcers of stability crumbled as individuality asserted itself. The heretics, iconoclasts, and sundry troublemakers, who had to face ostracism and death during the Middle Ages, became the heroes.

Clausewitz saw a similar transformation in war. War had remained medieval for centuries after the Renaissance had conquered the arts. Pitched battles hardly differed from the phalanxes employed by the Greeks. All focus was on tactics, the libretto of war, and the ultimate outcome was considered to be the ordainment of God. Clausewitz witnessed the rise and success of two seminal rule breakers: Frederick the Great of Prussia and Napoleon. They were preceded by lesser-known iconoclasts on the battlefield but were undoubtedly the first to employ the full resources of the emerging nation-state in war and for the purpose of a greater vision.

If it is reasonable to argue that if the Renaissance of business is now and in the immediate future, the words of Clausewitz must be appropriate preparation.

Strategy: Endgames Are Opening Games

A good game of chess, like a good story, has an opening phase, a middle game, and an endgame. As complicated as the game may be, this orderly succession of phases, with their own specific skills and arts, serves as reliable orientation for player, kibitzer, and theorist alike.

Business used to be similar. For endgames to emerge there must be firm rules and this was the case in the past. The initial phase of innovation was followed by emulation and intense competitive dynamics that, in turn, led to consolidation at the end of which a few near-monopolists or one de facto monopolist could claim the ultimate prize. This ultimate prize was in effect to have the game suspended and for the winner to enjoy the fruits of his investment uncontested.

Consumers and markets of today are no longer willing to grant this prize to winners, nor are competitors and start-ups as easily cowed into early capitulations. The rules that led to endgames no longer operate. Phenomenal riches, great influence, and outright adulation may all be fairly claimed as prizes by the best at the moment, but the ultimate prize of having the game stopped and victory be permanent will be denied no matter how great the investment and the exercise of talent. Consumers, competitors, and aspiring contestants all want the game to go on. The endgame is just the beginning of the next round.

Clausewitz's constant emphasis on strategy as the intelligent use of individual battles for the design of a sustainable campaign is remarkably relevant to the viewpoint that games in business are not confined in time and space. The husbandry of resources, the exercise of vision, the gathering of intelligence, and all other skills of heading a large organization can no longer be allowed to narrow down to the here and now, to the battle. We must learn to think in terms of never-ending campaigns and realize that unconditional efforts to become the winner at any given time and industry may just jeopardize one's chances in the next round. The sustainability of the campaign must be the focus of strategy.

The desire to win the endgame has been and continues to be the spiritual source of many mergers and acquisitions, and this may be a fateful error, as empirical evidence suggests. In the future, prospective partners in mergers may want to ask themselves—dialectically, so to speak—before the deal is consummated what they would need to be the agents of the new game rather than seeking the endgame in vain.

Competitors: Foe as Friend

It may well be very clear who is foe and who is friend in battle, and one is well advised to distinguish sharply between them. In the extended sweep of a campaign, however, the same sharp discrimination is more likely to obscure opportunities and lead to one's demise.

The vagaries caused by sharply reduced product development cycles, the imperative of marketing on a global scale, and the need for standards are among the most salient objective factors that have led former competitors to become allies in certain areas. But there is more to it than that. Any game that lets players forge and sever alliances as well as disrupt the alliances of others is richer and more exciting in strategic possibilities than a game that does not offer this freedom. In this sense, it is actually misleading to see in alliances a shift toward more cooperative and hence less competitive behavior. It is a shift toward a higher plane of competitive behavior.

Once leaders are accustomed to a slightly more dialectical point of view, the competitor emerges as mortal enemy now and as potential ally in the future or in another place. The converse may not be excluded either: The strategic mind must scan the logic of dumping current allies or being dumped by them. The strict separation between the polar opposites of friendship and enmity blurs, but the ambiguous middle ground is treacherous unless the mind retains the pure notions of the two extremes.

Customers: The Chameleon

There is no real equivalent for customers in war (if there were, we might not have wars), and it makes no sense to press Clausewitz into speaking of them. But the Clausewitzian method of exploration through opposites has been in use with regard to customers by the most innovative high-tech firms for two or three decades. These companies have known or discovered that the relationship with the customer lacks nothing in dialectical richness.

The customer as sovereign, king, or emperor has been found on closer inspection to be a less than benevolent ruler. Ignore your customers and you'll find yourself with no one to send bills to; pay close attention to them and react to their every whim and you may succeed in the tactics of the battle but not the strategy of the campaign. You'll never see the campaign because they—for sure—don't.

Listening to the customer is like listening to the past. Fair enough—the very recent past, but still, the past. To those who live further in the past this is a very good idea but those who are on the bleeding edge must have the courage to close their ears to the reality today and listen to their own intuition of the future.

Farewell to Tools

In its ultimate consequence, the philosophy of Clausewitz demands that commanders and executives not merely think when formulating strategy but that they arrive at a stage where they literally *think strategy*. The full meaning of this is at sharp odds with the notion of "tools" in strategy.

Even though the use of appropriate tools has become almost synonymous with good management, and their merits are incontestable in many areas, carrying the concept over into the realm of strategy has weakened the strategic spirit.

Clausewitz's denial of the positive doctrine in military strategy is a central recognition and a farewell to tools that must now also be embraced by business. The validity of a tool can reside only in its applicability to some class of stable phenomena in the past. In times of stability, all one needs to know is to trust the tool. In times of rapid change, that confidence is no longer warranted.

The Plasticity of Strategy

In business (and maybe also in military circles where Clausewitz is not always given the attention that he deserves) we have become accustomed to think of strategy as a *thing*. It is a thing that is designed, can be read, reviewed, revised and—most misleading—implemented. Companies are said to have one or be sadly lacking in one. There are those, of course, who emphasize strategy as a process but they too merely speak of a process (of planning) that results in this thing.

The careful reader of Clausewitz will discover that, although he often speaks of strategy as a substantive thing, this reification of strategy is contradicted by everything he has to say. In ultimate consequence, someone truly imbued with the teachings of Clausewitz must deny the existence of a thing called strategy.

Cognizant of the unsettled nature of the business environment as it is likely to develop in the near future, the question may arise legitimately whether it will be at all possible to craft strategies or whether we will be forced, in large part, to be content with tactical responses to fleeting opportunities as they emerge without advance notice. If strategy were truly the thing that the word suggests, one would have to respond affirmatively and strategy would degenerate into a clever, tactical sort of opportunism, but not much more.

Clausewitz would be the last to deny the enormous value—even decisiveness at times—that this latter sort of cleverness may have in certain situations and would rudely dismiss the conceited strategist who would dare to do so. Yet he would also vehemently argue that while in tactics we should exploit all opportunities that fortune offers with no regard to one's skills, preparation, and desires, in strategy we can combine moral fortitudes and mental aptitudes into a power of imagination and persuasion that creates opportunities in our favor and seduces fortune to take our side. In ultimate dialectical separation, focus on the purely tactical is a cynical surrender of the powers of individuals over their environment while exclusive reliance on strategy is blind ignorance of the forces that surround and oppose us. Opting for either is false. Opting for neither is also false. Constantly combining and recombining varying elements from both as reality unfolds, and as we force ourselves to perceive reality in clearer terms, is the Clausewitzian spirit of strategy.

Behind the apparent inconclusiveness of Clausewitzian thought is the endless plasticity of strategy, yet behind that plasticity is an iron, immutable resolve to demand the utmost of our moral forces and the free and creative powers of our minds.

Note to reader: At the end of each excerpt in the Clausewitz text, we include the page on which the excerpt can be found in the best known English and German versions of *On War.* The complete citations are in a footnote on page 52.

MARIE VON CLAUSEWITZ: PREFACE TO THE POSTHUMOUS EDITION (1832) OF HER HUSBAND'S WORKS, INCLUDING *ON WAR*

One might rightly be taken aback that a woman would dare write a preface for such a work as this. My friends will not require any explanation of my motives, but for those who do not know me, I hope to dispel any appearance of presumption on my part through this simple account of the reasons for my action.

The work for which these lines are to serve as an introduction occupied my indescribably beloved husband, who was taken far too soon from me and from the nation, almost exclusively for the last twelve years of his life. His dearest wish was to complete this work, but he did not intend to share it with the world during his lifetime. When I attempted to dissuade him from this course, his constant answer, given half in jest but half as well with a presentiment of an early death, was "*You* will publish it." In my friends' view, these words (which often elicited tears on my part, though I was little inclined at the time to take him seriously) now make it my duty to preface the works that my beloved husband left behind with these few lines. Although opinions may differ, certainly no one may misinterpret the emotion that has brought me to overcome the apprehension that makes it so difficult for a woman to appear in print, even in such an ancillary role.

Clearly it is not at all my intent to consider myself the actual editor of a work that lies far beyond the scope of my knowledge. I wish only to stand by this work as a participating companion, as it makes its way into the world. I am well positioned to play such a role, since I was allowed a similar one during its creation and development. Those who knew our blissful marriage and are aware of how we shared *everything* with each other—not just our joys and sufferings, but also every occupation, every element of daily life—will understand that a work of this nature could not have occupied my husband without also being equally well known to me. Therefore no one can bear witness as can I to the enthusiasm and love that he devoted to it, to the hopes he associated with it, and to the manner and time of its creation. From an early age, his richly endowed mind sensed a need for light and truth, and as broadly educated as he was, his thoughts focused mainly on military matters, to which his profession directed him, and which are of such significance for the welfare of nations. Scharnhorst was the first to point him along the right path, and his appointment in 1810 as an instructor at the General War College, and the honor accorded him at the same time of introducing His Royal Highness the Crown Prince to the study of war, provided him with new opportunities to direct his research and efforts along these lines, and to write down what he had worked out in his own mind.

An essay with which he concluded His Royal Highness the Crown Prince's instruction in 1812 already contains the seeds of his subsequent works. But it was not until 1816 in Koblenz that he once again began to concern himself with scholarly works, gathering together the fruits that his varied experiences in four critical years of war had yielded. He wrote down his views at first in brief essays that were only loosely related to each other. The following undated essay, which was found among his papers, appears to be from this early period:

> In my view, the statements written down here touch on the main topics of what is known as strategy. I considered them merely as draft materials, and had come pretty much to the point of bringing them together to form a single text.
>
> These drafts were written without a previously established plan. Initially my intent was to write down what I had thought out for myself in terms of the key points of this subject, in very brief, precise, succinct statements without regard to system or strict logical consistency. To some extent, I had in mind the approach that Montesquieu adopted for his subject. I felt that such brief, aphoristic chapters, which initially I wanted to call merely kernels, would appeal to intelligent readers just as much in terms of what could be developed

based on those ideas as in terms of what they stated directly. I had in mind, therefore, an intelligent reader who is already familiar with the subject. Yet my nature, which always drives me to develop and systematize things, ultimately expressed itself here, as well. For a while, I was able to lift out only the most important findings from the essays I wrote on particular topics in order to understand them clearly and fully, more narrowly focusing my thoughts in a smaller volume. Later, however, my customary habit got the better of me and I expanded the work as much as possible, thinking then, of course, of a reader not yet familiar with the subject.

The further I advanced in my work and the more I abandoned myself to the spirit of analysis, the more recourse I had to a systematic structure, and so gradually one chapter after another was added.

My ultimate intent was to review everything once again, expanding on the underlying reasoning in the earlier essays, and perhaps bringing together several analyses in the later essays into a single finding, thereby creating an acceptable whole that would form a small octavo volume. Here again, I wanted to avoid any sort of trite utterances, the sorts of self-evident things that have been said a hundred times over and are generally accepted. My ambition was to write a book that would not be forgotten in two or three years, one that someone interested in the topic could pick up more than once.

In Koblenz, where he had many official duties, he could devote only fragments of time to his private work. It was not until his appointment in 1818 as director of the General War College in Berlin that he had the free time to expand his work, and to enrich it with the history of more recent wars. This free time also reconciled him with his new post, which in other ways was not quite able to satisfy him, since, in accordance with the arrangements then in force at the War College, the scholarly portion of the institution was not under the responsibility of the director; rather, it was led by a special studies commission. Although he was free from any sort of petty self-importance, from any restless ambition, nonetheless he felt the need to be truly useful, and not to leave the talents that God had given him unused. In his work life, he was not in a position where this need could be met, and he held out little hope of ever obtaining such a post. So he devoted all his energies to scholarship, and his life's goal was the usefulness that he hoped to contribute through his work. His decision not to have the work published until after his death continued to grow stronger in him, proof enough that no vain desire for praise and recognition, no trace of any egotistical consideration, was mixed in with his honorable desire for great and long-lasting success.

So he continued working enthusiastically until he was transferred to the artillery in spring 1830. At that point, his work was devoted to an entirely different task, so much so that he had to give up on his literary activities at least for the time being. He arranged his papers, sealed them in individual packages, gave each one a label, and bid a sad farewell to this activity, which he held so dear. In August 1830 he was transferred to Breslau, where he was assigned to the Second Artillery Inspectorate, but by December he was called back to Berlin and appointed chief of staff to Field Marshal Count Gneisenau (for the duration of his command). In March 1831, he accompanied his commander, whom he admired, to Posen. When he returned from there to Breslau following his painful loss in November, he was cheered by the thought of being able to busy himself with his work, perhaps even completing it during the winter. God had other things in store: on November 7, he returned to Breslau, and died on the 16th. The packages that his hand had sealed were not opened until after his death!

It is these posthumous works that are now published in the following volumes, just exactly as they were found, without a word added or deleted. Still, publishing them entailed a great deal of work, much arranging and consultation. I owe a debt of thanks to many devoted friends who assisted me in this task, particularly to Major O'Etzel, who most kindly agreed to review the proofs and to prepare the maps that accompany the historical section of the work. I should also like to thank my beloved brother, who was my support in difficult times, and who in so many ways rendered such outstanding service with regard to this posthumous publication. Among other things, during his careful reading and arranging of the work, he discovered a revision of the work that my beloved husband had begun and mentioned in the *Note of 1827,* printed below, as a future project. He inserted the revisions in the parts of Book I for which they were intended (for that is as far as they went).

I should also like to thank many other friends for their counsel, for their support and friendship. Although I cannot mention them all by name, they can nonetheless be assured of my profound gratitude. My gratitude is all the greater because I am quite certain that everything they have done for me was not solely for my benefit, for also for that of their friend, whom God took from them too soon. For 21 years I was blissfully happy at the side of *such* a man. Despite my irreplaceable loss, I remain happy thanks to my treasured memories, my hopes, the rich legacy of support and friendship that I owe to my late beloved husband, and the uplifting sense that his unique worth is now so generally and so honorably recognized.

The trust that brought a noble prince and princess to call me to their service is a new kindness for which I thank God,★ as it opens up to me an honorable undertaking to which I gladly devote myself. May this undertaking be blessed, and may the dear little prince now entrusted to my care one day read this book, and be inspired by it to accomplish deeds similar to those of his glorious forebears!

★She had been appointed as Governess to Prince Friedrich Wilhelm, who later became Emperor Frederick III.

Written at the Marble Palace at Potsdam, June 30, 1832.

Marie von Clausewitz,
Born Countess Brühl,
First Lady in Waiting to Her Royal Highness,
Princess Wilhelm.★

★Among Prussian aristocrats, a wife would often take the first name of her husband, much as the wife of John Smith may be known as Mrs. John Smith in the English-speaking world.

THE GENIUS OF STRATEGY

*In which an uncompromising theorist delivers a mortal blow
to the hollow core of pretentious theorizing
and pays ultimate tribute to the supremacy of practical talent.*

*The author, as if inspired by the marketing spirit of later ages,
starts with the simplest of questions:
Whom should systematic reflection on practice serve other than
the practitioners of greatest talent, those of genius—
if we accept that nothing can replace genius?*

*Guided by appreciation of what talent can accomplish
if liberated from the shackles of false doctrines,
the author arrives at a concept of theory
to serve genius rather than usurp its rightful primacy.*

The Coup d'Oeil

GENIUS AND DISCRETION IN JUDGMENT

Each particular activity, if it is to be performed with a certain amount of virtuosity, requires specific aptitudes of the mind and heart. When these qualities are present to an exceptional degree and are demonstrated through extraordinary achievements, the term *genius* is used to describe the mind to which they belong.

Of course, this word is used with a great variety of meanings, and for many of these meanings, defining the essence of genius is very difficult indeed. But since we do not claim to be experts in philosophy or language, we may be permitted to adhere to a meaning that is familiar to us from common usage, understanding the term *genius* to denote a greatly enhanced mental aptitude for certain activities.

I should like for a few moments to dwell on this faculty, the dignity of the mind, to ascertain its validity in greater detail and to understand the term more fully. But in doing so we cannot limit ourselves to genius per se, as a highly developed talent, since that notion does not have any measurable boundaries. We must focus instead on the concerted application of intellectual forces as they pertain to military activities, which we may then consider the *essence of military genius*. We have said the *concerted* application, because the military genius specifically is not constituted by a single suitable ability, such as courage, for example, to the exclusion of other abilities of the mind and heart. Rather, the military genius is a *harmonious conjunction of abilities,* in which one or another may stand out, but none may conflict with the others. (H&P 100; H 231–232)*

If we look more closely at the demands that war places on those involved in it, we find that *intellectual powers predominate*. War is the realm of uncertainty. Three-fourths of the elements on which action in war is based lie in a fog of greater or lesser uncertainty. Here, first of all, sensitive and penetrating intellectual power is required to feel out the truth using one's instinctual intelligence.

An average mind may sometimes happen across this truth, and uncommon courage may compensate for an error on other occasions, but the majority of instances, the average outcome, will always expose imperfect intelligence.

War is the province of chance. In no other human activity must so much leeway be allowed for this intruder, because no other human activity is in such close contact with it at every turn. Chance increases the uncertainty of all circumstances, upsetting the course of events.

The uncertainty of all reports and suppositions and the constant interference of chance mean that the person acting in war at every instant finds that matters are different from what he had

---

*For those who would like to explore *On War* in its entirety, at the end of each selection we indicate the page on which the excerpt can be found in the complete Michael Howard and Peter Paret edition (Princeton, NJ: Princeton University Press, 1989) and, in German, in the complete Werner Hahlweg edition, *Vom Kriege: Hinterlassenes Werk des Generals Carl von Clausewitz,* 19th ed. (Bonn: Ferd. Dümmlers Verlag, 1991).

expected; this necessarily will have an impact on his plans, or at the very least on his thinking about those plans. If this influence is significant enough for him to call off what he intended to do, new plans must generally be devised in their stead. Often, information for these new plans is lacking, because as the action progresses, circumstances render the decision urgent, leaving no time to reassess the situation. It is much more common, however, that corrections of what we had in mind and knowledge of chance happenings are not enough to reverse our plans entirely, but merely render them unsteady. Our knowledge of the situation has been enhanced, but this increases rather than decreases our uncertainty. The reason is that these experiences do not come all at once, but gradually, besieging our decisions constantly; the mind, so to speak, must be under arms at all times.

If the mind is to survive this constant battle with the unexpected, two qualities are indispensable: *first, an intellect that even in this moment of intense darkness retains some trace of the inner light that will lead it to the truth, and second, the courage to go where that faint light leads.* The first is metaphorically described by the French term *coup d'oeil* [a glance or look], the second is *determination*. (H&P 101–102; H 233–234)

Since battles are first and foremost among the things that draw attention in war, and time and space are key elements in battles (particularly back when the cavalry and its rapid decision-making were the main thing), the concept of the rapid and accurate decision emerged initially from estimating both of these elements. Subsequently, the term that came to be used to designate this action relates only to having a good eye for distances.

As a result, many teachers of the art of war have defined that term in keeping with this limited meaning. However, it is noteworthy that the term soon came to be applied to all accurate decisions made in the heat of the moment, for example, recognizing the right place for the attack, etc. Therefore, the term *coup d'oeil* commonly refers not merely to physical sight, but to intellectual vision, as well. Of course the term, like the quality itself, has always been right at home in the field of tactics, but it can apply to strategy as well, since strategy also often requires that decisions be made quickly. If we strip the term of metaphor and the limitations imposed on it by the expression itself, the *coup d'oeil* proves to be nothing more than the rapid recognition of a truth that is utterly invisible to the ordinary view of the mind, or becomes visible only after protracted thought and reflection. (H&P 102; H 235)

Here, then, the action of the intellect leaves the realm of the exact sciences, logic and mathematics. It enters that of art in the broadest sense, that is, skill in discerning, from a mass of countless objects and relations, what is most important and decisive through the discrimination of judgment. Without question, this power of judgment consists more or less of an instinctive comparison of all forces and relationships, during which the most remote and unimportant are quickly set aside and the more immediate and important are identified more quickly than if logical deduction had been applied.

Therefore, in order to discover the extent of the means needed for war, we must consider the political goal to be achieved on our side and on the enemy's. We must take into consideration the abilities and situation of the enemy state and of our own. We must consider the character of its government and its people, and the capabilities of both, and we must do the same for our side. We must consider the political connections of other states, and the effects that war may have upon them. It is easy to see that sifting through all these manifold and intertwining elements is a vast undertaking, that it takes a true flash of genius to quickly light on the right answer, and that it would be utterly impossible to master this multiplicity of factors through some type of schoolroom deliberation.

To be sure, the sheer variety and number of conditions make a favorable outcome considerably more difficult. But we must not

Penetrating Uncertainty

Helmuth von Moltke (1800–1891), possibly the most committed disciple of Clausewitz, and by many considered the most brilliant military man since Napoleon, headed the Prussian and German General Staff from 1858 to 1888. In *On Strategy* he wrote:

> No plan of operations extends with certainty beyond the first encounter with the enemy's main strength. Only the layman sees in the course of a campaign a consistent execution of a preconceived and highly detailed original concept pursued consistently to the end.
>
> Certainly the commander in chief will keep his great objective continuously in mind, undisturbed by the vicissitudes of events. But the path on which he hopes to reach it can never be firmly established in advance. Throughout the campaign he must make a series of decisions on the basis of situations that cannot be foreseen. The successive acts of war are thus not premeditated designs, but on the contrary are spontaneous acts guided by military measures. Everything depends on penetrating the uncertainty of veiled situations to evaluate the facts, to clarify the unknown, to make decisions rapidly, and then to carry them out with strength and constancy.

overlook the enormous and incomparable *importance* of the issue, which though it does not increase the complexity and difficulty of the task, does increase the value of the solution. The average person does not respond to danger and responsibility with renewed intellectual vigor and a sense of liberation—quite the opposite. So when those conditions strengthen a person's judgment and set it soaring, we can be sure that the person is one of extraordinary greatness. (H&P 585–586; H 961–962)

COURAGE AND DETERMINATION

War is the realm of danger, and therefore courage, above all else, is the first quality of the warrior. Courage is twofold: courage in the face of personal danger, and courage in the face of responsibility, either in the court of some external authority or before an internal one, namely the conscience. Only the first of these is discussed here.

Courage in the face of personal danger is itself twofold. First, courage may be indifferent in the face of danger, whether that indifference derives from the individual's particular nature, disregard for life, or force of habit—but, in any event, it must be considered a permanent condition. Second, courage may derive from such positive motives as ambition, patriotism, or enthusiasm of some sort. In this case, courage is not so much a condition as an emotion, a feeling.

It is understandable that the two types differ in their effect. The first type is reliable, because it never abandons the individual once it has become second nature. The second type often leads further. The first is closer to steadfastness, the second to boldness. The first leaves the mind clearer, the second arouses it, but often may also blind it. The two joined together yield the most complete sort of courage. (H&P 101; H 233)

Determination is an act of courage in a particular instance, and if it becomes characteristic, it is a mental habit. But what is at issue is not courage in the face of physical danger, but rather in terms of shouldering responsibility, specifically moral danger. This has often been called *courage d'esprit* because it springs from the intellect. Yet this courage is not an act of the mind, but an act of the heart. Intellect alone is not courage, because we often see the brightest people unsure of themselves. Intellect, therefore, must first stir the feeling of courage in order to be sustained and borne by it, for in the urgency of the moment feelings have a stronger hold over men than does thought.

Clausewitz on Scharnhorst

The following obituary was written by Clausewitz in 1813 after the death of his longtime teacher, mentor, friend, and patron, Lieutenant-General Gerhard Scharnhorst, and appeared in *Die Befreiund*. Scharnhorst was perhaps the most influential soldier in the Prussian army during the Napoleonic era; his name above all others is associated with the far-reaching military reforms undertaken by the Prussians to rehabilitate their army after its defeat by Napoleon in 1806. Scharnhorst was also a fearless and capable leader in combat, ultimately dying of wounds he sustained in battle against the French. Clausewitz's description of Scharnhorst—here, and also in a biographical sketch he wrote in 1817—paints an implicit portrait of a military genius realized in a living being: a man who combined a brilliant and independent intellect, a strong psychology, personal courage, and the ability to execute.

On June 28, Royal Prussian Lieutenant-General Scharnhorst died in Prague from wounds received in the battle at Grossgörschen. He was one of the most outstanding men of our age. His tireless, steady, methodical pursuit of his goals, the clarity and steadfastness of his intellect, the comprehensive scope of his views, his freedom from prejudice with respect to one's origins, his proud indifference to external honors, his courage to strive for the greatest goals through the sheer strength of his spirit, under the most improbable conditions and using the simplest of means, his youthful entrepreneurial spirit, his circumspection, courage, and fortitude in the face of danger, and finally his comprehensive understanding of warfare, make him one of the most remarkable statesmen and soldiers of whom Germany has ever been proud.

Fair-minded and impartial in his judgments, gentle and quiet in his relationships with others, friendly, sincere in all his dealings, temperate and honorable in his sensitivity towards others, he was one of the most charming men ever to grace the social circles.

Thus we place determination in a position where its role is to relieve the torments of doubt and the dangers of procrastination when motives for action are inadequate.

The determination that wins out over a doubtful situation can be derived only through the intellect, and indeed, only through a very particular sort of intellect. We maintain that the mere coexistence of higher insights and the necessary feelings are still not enough to give rise to determination. Some people have outstanding intellectual capacity for the most difficult tasks, people with the courage to tackle a great many things, but who are incapable of reaching a decision when the situation becomes difficult. Their courage and their insight are isolated from each other; they do not reach out to each other, and therefore fail to produce determination as a third quality. That determination comes about only through an act of the intellect, which brings the need for daring into the consciousness, thereby lending shape to the will. It is this very particular orientation of the intellect, in which the fear of hesitation and delay overrides all other human fears, that creates determination in strong hearts. That is why people of little intellect cannot have determination as we have defined it. In difficult situations, they may act without delay, but they do so without reflection, and obviously those who act without consideration cannot be torn apart by doubt. This approach may well find the right way now and then, but I shall repeat what I said previously: It is the average result that proves the existence of a military genius. (H&P 102–103; H 235–236)

We believe that determination owes its existence to a particular direction of the mind, specifically to one that belongs more to a strong mind than a brilliant one. We can provide further evidence of this lineage of determination by citing the many examples of men who showed the greatest determination in lower positions only to lose it in higher ones. Although they are aware of the need to make a decision, they also see the dangers lurking in a *wrong* decision, and since they are unfamiliar with the issues they now face, their intelligence loses its original strength. They become increasingly hesitant as they become more aware of the dangers inherent in the failure to reach a decision, and in proportion to how accustomed they had been to acting on the spur of the moment. (H&P 103; H 236–237)

DISTILLING EXPERIENCE

The commander need not be a learned statesman or historian, nor even a political commentator; however, he must be quite conversant with the higher matters of state and customary practices, and he must know and correctly assess the interests at stake, the issues of the day, and the players involved. He need not be an excellent observer of men, nor need he be able to analyze the human character in painstaking detail, but he must know the character, mind-set, and manners, as well as the usual failings and preferences, of those he is to lead. He need not know anything about fitting out a wagon or harnessing horses for the artillery, but he must know how to correctly determine how long a column will take to march under various conditions.

This knowledge is not something that can be forced from a construct of scientific formulas and mechanisms; it can be acquired only if appropriate judgment is exercised in analyzing these issues in real life, and if a talented mind is devoted to this task.

The knowledge needed for high-level military activity is characterized by the fact that it takes a particular talent to acquire it, through reflection, study, and thought; this unique talent is an intellectual instinct that is capable of drawing out the essence of real events just as a bee draws honey from the flowers. In addition to reflection and study, this knowledge also comes from life itself. Life, with its wealth of lessons, will never produce a Newton or an Euler, but it will yield the higher calculus of a Condé or a Frederick.

F. Scott Fitzgerald on Opposed Ideas

F. Scott Fitzgerald's famous essay of the late 1930s, "The Crack-Up," offers a rich description of the string of depressions and nervous break-downs that gradually made the author relinquish "the old dream of being an entire man." Though at the time of writing, Fitzgerald sees himself as a "sombre literary man writing pieces upon the state of emotional exhaustion that often overtakes writers in their prime," his account also recalls his youthful determination to succeed. The writer's awareness of a young man's need to grapple with discordant ideas and yet pursue a course of action distinctly echoes Clausewitz's thoughts of genius, intellect, and perseverance.

Before I go on with this short history, let me make a general observation—the test of a first-rate intelligence is the ability to hold two opposed ideas in the mind at the same time, and still retain the ability to function. One should, for example, be able to see that things are hopeless and yet be determined to make them otherwise. This philosophy fitted on to my early adult life, when I saw the improbable, the implausible, often the "impossible," come true. Life was something you dominated if you were any good. Life yielded easily to intelligence and effort, or to what proportion could be mustered of both.

To rescue the intellectual dignity of military activity, it is unnecessary to resort to untruths and simplistic pedantry. There has never been an outstanding commander of limited intellectual gifts. Yet there have been many cases of individuals who served with great distinction in lower ranks only to perform in a mediocre manner upon promotion to a higher rank, because their intellectual talents were inadequate. Clearly, a distinction must also be made among the ranks of commanders in accordance with their level of authority. (H&P 146–147; H 298–299)

GENIUS IN ACTION

The commander also becomes a statesman, but he should not cease being a commander. On the one hand, he is thoroughly familiar with the political situation; on the other hand, he knows exactly what he can achieve with the means at his disposal.

The diversity and fluid boundaries of [political and military] conditions entail a great many factors that must be considered, and the only way to assess most of these factors is according to the laws of probability. Accordingly, the person acting in war must comprehend all this from the viewpoint of a mind that senses the truth in all things, for otherwise such a confusion of considerations and views would arise that his judgment would be unable to sort them all out.

The higher powers of the mind required here are unity and judgment, raised to a wondrous pitch of vision that readily touches on and sets aside a thousand half-obscure notions that a more common intellect would bring to light only with enormous effort, and that would become exhausted in the process. But this higher mental activity, this view of the genius, would not be of historical importance unless it is supported by the qualities of temperament and character that we have discussed previously.

Truth alone is a feeble motivator of men's actions, and there is always a sharp distinction between cognition and volition, between knowing what to do and being able to do it. The strongest motivation for action always comes from the emotions, the most powerful backing, if we may use that expression, from the amalgamation of temperament and intellect which we have come to recognize in resolution, firmness, steadfastness, and strength of character.

However, if this lofty activity of the mind and heart of the commander were not evident in the ultimate success of his actions, and were merely accepted as an article of faith, it would almost never rise to the level of historical significance.

Finally then, if we wish, without venturing to define the higher powers of the spirit, to assert that there are differences in intellectual powers, as is commonly believed and reflected in the language, and if we were to ask what sort of intellect is most closely associated with military genius, observation and experience inform us that it is the analytical rather than the creative mind, the more all-encompassing than the narrowly focused mind, the cooler rather than the hot-tempered mind that we should more readily entrust in war with the well-being of our brothers and children, and the honor and safety of our country. (H&P 111–112; H 251–252)

Theory in the
Service of Genius

THE TROUBLE WITH THEORY

When, on the one hand, we see how military action seems so very simple, when we hear and read how the greatest commanders speak about it in the simplest and plainest terms, how—in their mouths—the governance and movement of that ponderous machine made up of a hundred thousand parts sounds no more complicated than if they were discussing their own person, so that the whole immense act of war is individualized into a sort of one-on-one combat; when, in this process, the motives of their action are reported now through a few simple ideas, now through some stirring of the soul; when we see the easy, confident, one might even say casual way in which they regard the whole matter—and then, on the other hand, when we see the number of circumstances that are suggested to the inquiring intellect, the vast, often limitless horizons toward which the individual threads lead, and the huge number of combinations that lie before us, and in so doing when we think of the obligation of theory to present these things with clarity and thoroughness, and always to lead each action back to a necessary and adequate cause, we are overcome by the fear of being dragged down by some irresistible force to the level of pedantry, to crawl around in the depths of cumbersome concepts where we will never encounter the great commander, with his straightforward viewpoint. If that is the outcome of theoretical efforts, it would be just as well, or even better, never to have engaged in them in the first place.

Such theorizing is of little interest to talented individuals, and it is soon forgotten. On the other hand, this straightforward viewpoint of the commander, this simple way of presenting matters, this personification of the whole undertaking of war, is the very core of good generalship. It is only in this splendid way that the mind achieves the freedom it needs to be the master of events, and not to be overpowered by them. (H&P 577–578; H 950–951)

In times past, the terms *art of war* and *science of war* were always taken as referring exclusively to knowledge and skills as they relate to material objects. The objects of this knowledge and these skills were the fitting out, preparation, and use of weapons, the construction of fortifications and fieldworks, the structuring of the army and the mechanisms of its movements. They all led to the production of armed forces that were useful in war. The whole approach focused on material issues, a one-sided activity, essentially just an activity that rose gradually from the level of a trade to that of a refined mechanical art. This was no more applicable to war than the swordsmith's art is to fencing. There was no consideration yet of using the actual stirrings of intellect and courage in times of danger, amid constant interactions, to achieve a larger objective.

Later on, in the mechanics of all the elements it brings together, tactics sought to establish a general procedure based on the particular properties of the instrument. This was certainly suitable for the battlefield, but not for unfettered intellectual activity. Rather, it resulted in an army transformed through formation and battle order into an automaton that was supposed to carry out its activities like clockwork merely upon receiving its orders. (H&P 133; H 279–280)

Indeterminacy and Freedom

Leo Tolstoy — *War and Peace;* book 13, chapter VII

No battle—Tarutino, Borodino, or Austerlitz—takes place as those who planned it anticipated. That is an essential condition.

A countless number of free forces (for nowhere is man freer than during a battle, where it is a question of life and death) influence the course taken by the fight, and that course never can be known in advance and never coincides with the direction of any one force. If many simultaneously and variously directed forces act on a given body, the direction of its motion cannot coincide with any one of those forces, but will always be a mean—what in mechanics is represented by the diagonal of a parallelogram of forces. If in the descriptions given by historians, especially French ones, we find their wars and battles carried out in accordance with previously formed plans, the only conclusion to be drawn is that those descriptions are false.

Tolstoy and Clausewitz share a great understanding of the dynamics of battle and the resulting indeterminacy of the chain of events. Their common interpretation arose neither out of irrational thinking nor out of mysticism, although each of them has been accused of one tendency or the other, but from thoughtful observation of the difference between what should happen and what really does happen. Both distrust the retrospective rationalization of events, and both are capable of using the language of science to make their points forcefully (the motion described here by Tolstoy, for example, would be described as Brownian motion in our days).

Tolstoy presents a remarkable thesis: that man attains his greatest freedom in battle. Ironically, few people find themselves in battle through their own free will, and most of their actions there are theoretically determined by the commands of superiors, yet once the battle has begun, the immediacy of mortal danger overrides all other considerations.

In the less sanguine setting of sports and the performing arts, psychological studies have revealed that accomplished athletes and artists experience a sensation of complete freedom when driven to the heights of their capabilities by competitors or the expectations of a demanding audience; likewise, the most demanding, dynamic, and competitive industries succeed best at attracting and retaining top talent. High salaries are not a sufficient explanation, since businesspeople often speak of the *thrill* that attracts them and propels them to give up many other things that they cherish. That thrill may come very close to what Tolstoy describes as freedom—although if free will exists only in situations with some room for decision, those freedoms of choice, imagination, and talent are also inevitably subject to the influence of chance.

The active management of war, that is, the unrestricted use of prepared means in a way tailored to meet specific requirements, was thought to be an inappropriate subject for theory; rather, it was to be left up to natural abilities. Slowly, as war was transformed from the hand-to-hand combat of the Middle Ages into a more regular and structured form, the human mind did have to grapple with some considerations in this regard. Yet these ruminations generally occurred in passing in memoirs and histories, and to some extent appeared incognito.

As these reflections became more and more numerous, and the telling of history grew more critical, an urgent need arose for a set of principles and rules so that the conflicts of opinion that are so natural in the field of military history could be brought to some resolution. This furor of opinions, spinning without fixed reference and not guided by any perceptible rules, was sure to be offensive to the human mind.

So an effort was made to set up principles, rules, or even entire systems for the management of war. This constituted a positive goal, but the infinite difficulties that the management of war poses in this respect were not taken into due account. As we have noted,

---

Deferral of Closure

American philosopher and educator Susanne Langer (1895–1985) drew from philosophy, aesthetics, biology, biochemistry, psychology, and other disciplines in her writings on linguistic analysis and aesthetics. She recognizes that researchers (the leaders in their fields) want to be in a state of certainty about the phenomena they investigate even though that certainty is impossible. The framework she proposes for understanding the human mind is similar in spirit to the approach taken by Clausewitz for elucidating the nature of strategy.

[Many scientists and philosophers try] to define the subject matter of psychology, in the belief that if we knew exactly what we are dealing with we could apply scientific methods to this material and thus find the basic laws which govern it, as physicists have done in their proper realm.

But it may be questioned whether this is really a profitable approach. The precise definition of the matter and scope of a science is more likely to become accessible in the course of intimate study, as more and more becomes known about it, than to be its first step. Physics did not begin with a clear concept of "matter"—that concept is still changing rapidly with the advance of knowledge. . . . What we need for a science of mind is not so much a definitive concept of mind, as a conceptual frame in which to lodge our observations of mental phenomena.

---

the management of war runs off in nearly all directions, and does so without limitation. Yet every system, every edifice for teaching, possesses the inherent limitations of synthesis. Therefore, there is an irreconcilable conflict between such a theory and reality itself.

However, theorists soon became aware of the difficulty of their task, and felt justified in sidestepping difficulty by focusing their principles and systems once again on material objects alone, and on one-sided activity. As in the sciences relating to the *preparation for war*, they wanted merely to reach certain positive results, thus taking into account only those things that could be the object of calculations. (H&P 134; H 280–281)

Failed Theories

Numerical Superiority. Numerical superiority was a material thing, and it was singled out from among all the factors in the product of victory because it could be fitted into a system of mathematical laws through a combination of time and space considerations. It was believed that all other circumstances could be ignored, since they were believed to be the same on both sides, effectively canceling each other out. That would have been useful if the intent were to do so temporarily, in order to examine the conditions affecting that one factor. But to do so permanently, to hold that numerical superiority is the only rule, and to believe that the whole secret of the art of war could be summed up as *having numerical superiority in particular places at a particular time,* was a limitation that could never withstand the force of reality.

Base. One ingenious thinker attempted to sum up a broad range of factors, some of which were in fact linked through intellectual bonds, in the single concept of the *base*. These factors included *feeding the army, supplementing the army and its equipment, ensuring the security of its communications with the home country,* and finally, *ensuring the security of its retreat,* if necessary.

At first, he tried to substitute this concept for all the individual elements, and then to substitute the size (extent) of the base for the base itself, and finally to substitute the angle the armed forces formed with the base for the size of the base. All of this effort was expended to come up with a purely geometrical result that is utterly worthless. This worthlessness actually comes as no surprise, if one recalls that none of those substitutions could be made without inflicting harm on the truth, and omitting some of the things that were still encompassed within the preceding concept. The concept of a base is vital for strategy, and it is a great contribution to have come up with the idea. But using that concept as we have described above is completely impermissible, and inevitably led to entirely one-sided results that, indeed, impelled these theorists in an utterly absurd direction, namely toward proclaiming the superior effectiveness of the enveloping attack.

Slide-Rule Theorists Then and Now

Leo Tolstoy—*War and Peace;* book 9, chapter IX

General Headquarters of the Russian army—June 1812, Drissa

The adjutants general were there because they always accompanied the Emperor, and lastly and chiefly Pfuel was there because he had drawn up the plan of campaign against Napoleon and, having induced Alexander to believe in the efficacy of that plan, was directing the whole business of the war. With Pfuel was Wolzogen, who expressed Pfuel's thoughts in a more comprehensible way than Pfuel himself (who was a harsh, bookish theorist, self-confident to the point of despising everyone else) was able to do.

Besides these Russians and foreigners who propounded new and unexpected ideas every day—especially the foreigners, who did so with a boldness characteristic of people employed in a country not their own—there were many secondary personages accompanying the army because their principals were there.

Among the opinions and voices in this immense, restless, brilliant, and proud sphere, Prince Andrew noticed the following sharply defined subdivisions and parties:

The first party consisted of Pfuel and his adherents—military theorists who believed in a science of war with immutable laws— laws of oblique movements, outflankings, and so forth. Pfuel and his adherents demanded a retirement into the depths of the country in accordance with precise laws defined by a pseudo-theory of war, and they saw only barbarism, ignorance, or evil intention in every deviation from that theory. To this party belonged the foreign nobles, Wolzogen, Wintzingerode, and others, chiefly Germans.

book 9, chapter X

At first sight, Pfuel, in his ill-made uniform of a Russian general, which fitted him badly like a fancy costume, seemed familiar to Prince Andrew, though he saw him now for the first time. There was about him something of Weyrother, Mack, and Schmidt, and many other German theorist-generals whom Prince Andrew had seen in 1805, but he was more typical than any of them. Prince Andrew had never yet seen a German theorist in whom all the characteristics of those others were united to such an extent.

Pfuel was short and very thin but broad-boned, of coarse, robust build, broad in the hips, and with prominent shoulder blades. His face was much wrinkled and his eyes deep set. His hair had evidently been hastily brushed smooth in front of the temples, but stuck up behind in quaint little tufts. He entered the room, looking restlessly and angrily around, as if afraid of everything in that large apartment. Awkwardly holding up his sword, he addressed Chernyshev and asked in German where the Emperor was. One could see that he wished to pass through the rooms as quickly as possible, finish with the bows and greetings, and sit down to business in front of a map, where he would feel at home. He nodded hurriedly in reply to Chernyshev, and smiled ironically on hearing that the sovereign was inspecting the fortifications that he, Pfuel, had planned in accord with his theory. He muttered something to himself abruptly and in a bass voice, as self-assured Germans do—it might have been "stupid fellow" . . . or "the whole affair will be ruined," or "something absurd will come of it." . . . Prince Andrew did not catch what he said and would have passed on, but Chernyshev introduced him to Pfuel, remarking that Prince Andrew was just back from Turkey where the war had terminated so fortunately. Pfuel barely glanced—not so much at Prince Andrew as past him—and said, with a laugh: "That must have been a fine tactical war"; and, laughing contemptuously, went on into the room from which the sound of voices was heard.

Tolstoy's vitriolic portrayal of Pfuel, other theorists of war, and Germans is starkly and darkly colored by his philosophy of history and his passionate rejection of the teachings of Hegel, which—to the horror of Tolstoy—had an enormous influence in certain circles of the Russian intelligentsia at the time that he was writing *War and Peace*. Although a caricature and unjust in its generalizations, Clausewitz would have agreed in substance. Tolstoy and Clausewitz shared a deep distrust of false theorizing.

Both would have objected to the blind reliance on the predictive power of theory and both would have agreed that the dynamic nature of war voids all attempts at prediction.

More than a century later the "theorists of oblique movements," while no longer preaching oblique movements, were still present, influential, and as smugly self-confident as ever. In the aftermath of the Vietnam War they were caricatured in terms no less harsh than Tolstoy had for Pfuel as "slide-rule strategists."

Interior Lines. As a reaction against this erroneous belief, another geometrical principle, namely that of the *interior line,* was then proclaimed. However, even though this principle is based on solid ground, namely that battle is the only truly effective means in war, its purely geometrical nature makes it just one more one-sided approach that could never hold sway in real life.

Pitfalls. It is only the analytical parts of all these attempted theories that can be considered advances in the realm of truth; they are utterly useless in their synthetic efforts, in their rules and regulations. They strive for definite values while everything in war is indefinite and all calculations rest on nothing but variable quantities. They focus solely on material values, while the whole military act is interwoven with intellectual forces and effects. They consider only unilateral action, whereas war is a constant interaction of opposites. (H&P 136, H 283–284)

Everything that could not be attained by the scanty wisdom of a one-sided perspective lay beyond the domain of science, and constituted the realm of genius, *which rises above the rules.*

Woe betide the warrior who had to crawl around in this wretched collection of rules that are not good enough for genius, and that distinguished genius can disregard or hold up for ridicule! What genius actually does must be deemed the best rule. Theory can do nothing better than to point out how and why that is so.

Woe betide the theory that stands in opposition to the intellect; it can never overcome such a contradiction through humility, and the more humble it is, the faster derision and contempt will drive it out of real life. (H&P 134–136, H 281–284)

A Positive Doctrine Is Inconceivable. Given the nature of the matter at hand, we must recall that it would be utterly impossible to attempt to set up a sort of structural framework for the art of war, in the form of a positive doctrinal edifice, that would provide external support in every situation for a person acting in war. Every time that person relies on his own talent, he finds himself outside the edifice, and indeed in conflict with it. No matter how versatile the construct, the outcome that we have already discussed will always come to pass: *Talent and genius act outside limited, artificial rules, and theory conflicts with reality.* (H&P 140; H 289)

The Disrupture of Rules

Businesspeople are well aware of the value of breaking the rules of established business wisdom. Business innovations can hardly fail to break with the past and lead to new rules. The ensuing transformation of industry by new rules of the game is rightly considered an integral part of strategy. The iconoclasts of business—those who have successfully broken with the rules of the past—have set new technical standards or established new business models or created whole new product categories. They are almost invariably newcomers to their industry because breaking rules and thus defying existing beliefs is the hardest for those who have established and benefited from them.

Clausewitz formulated his reflections on rules, genius, and the role of theory with an ironic undertone that is easily missed or misinterpreted. The primary target of his criticism is conventional theory and its practitioners. They are satisfied with codifying the existing rules as permanent and immutable features of theory and are thus forced to view the breaking of rules as an act of mysterious origin and inspiration that must remain inexplicable within theory and therefore reside outside it. Conventional theories opt for the relative ease of expounding the static logic of current rules at the expense of shedding light on the dynamic nature of rules, which is much harder for theory to capture. The *genius* of conventional theory is an escape clause to be invoked when theory is obviously about to fail—it is a *deus ex machina*. Not so for Clausewitz.

In Clausewitzian thought, any valid theory must necessarily include intelligent provisions for the continuous emergence of new concepts and behaviors that defy existing rules. Theory may not simply shun these discontinuities as something hard to deal with (which they are) but must accept as essential features of strategic reality both the disrupture of rules and the genius as the agent of disrupture. Clausewitz realizes that by allowing discontinuities to reside within the body of his theory, theory must abandon the narrow, pedantic, and ultimately vacuous claim of having a neat explanation for everything. Good theory must recognize that it cannot foresee all that human ingenuity may bring forth, but nonetheless must anticipate their inevitable emergence and encapsulate the driving mechanism of disrupture. Clausewitz was both an observant eyewitness of revolutionary changes in warfare and a keen student of history, and as such he understood both the advantages and limitations of innovation. Of the brilliantly successful "emerging technologies" of Napoleonic warfare, he remarked: "These new tools were a natural and necessary outcome of the obsolescence of traditional structures." Conscious of the extent to which innovation is only part of the strategic game, Clausewitz continued his comments on the advantages of the new forms of war by pointing out that they "increased the strength of those who used them first to such an extent that the opponent was swept along and had to adopt them, as well." (H&P 479; H 799–800)

Thus an innovator may enjoy the initial advantages of novelty—but those advantages are inherently transient, lasting only as long as it takes the competition to recognize and adopt them.

THEORY AS AN AID TO JUDGMENT

All the positive results of theoretical investigation, all principles, rules, and methods, increasingly lack universality and absolute truth the more they become a positive doctrine. They are there to present themselves for use. Judgment must always be free to determine whether or not they are suitable. Criticism must never use these results of theory as laws and standards, but only as a person acting in war should also do: as *aids to judgment.*

Although it is commonly accepted in the realm of tactics that in the general battle order the cavalry should not ride alongside, but rather behind, the infantry, it would be foolish to rule out any arrangement that differs from this. The critic should study the reasons for the variation, and only if those reasons prove inadequate does he then have the right to refer to the findings of theory. Moreover, if it is accepted in theory that an attack with divided forces reduces the chances for success, it would be equally unreasonable, in every instance where an attack with divided forces met with failure, to conclude without further investigation that the failure was the result of that approach. Likewise, whenever such an attack and a successful outcome occurred together, it would be unreasonable to conclude that the theoretical assertion was incorrect. The inquiring mind of the critic must not permit either to occur. Therefore, criticism relies mainly on the results of the analytical investigation of the theorist. What theory has concluded need not be arrived at once again from scratch. Theory must see to it that the critic is provided with these findings. (H&P 157–158; H 315)

Theory should illuminate all things, so that the intellect can more readily find its way; theory should tear out the weeds that error has strewn about; theory should reveal the relationships among things, separating what is important from what is not. Where concepts combine of their own accord to form that core of truth we call a principle, where they follow a pattern that forms a rule, theory should make that evident.

What the mind takes from these subterranean wanderings among fundamental concepts, what illumination the mind gains, is in fact what is practical about theory. Theory cannot provide the mind with formulae for resolving specific tasks; it cannot limit the mind's path to a narrow line of inevitable action in accordance with principles that it lines up on either side. . . . Theory enables the mind to have insight into the great number of phenomena and their interrelationships, and leaves the mind on its own once again in the higher regions of action. There, in accordance with its natural abilities, it may act, joining all these abilities together and becoming conscious of what is *true* and what is *right,* as though becoming conscious of a single clear idea that, through the combined pressure of all these abilities, appears to be more a product of a perceived threat than the product of thought. (H&P 578; H 951)

Theory does not necessarily have to be a positive doctrine or *set of instructions* for action. Wherever an action deals for the most part repeatedly with the same matters, with the same objectives and means—even though there may be some small changes from one situation to another, and even if those changes may occur in a vast number of combinations—these matters must be capable of being studied rationally. Indeed, such an examination is the key part of any *theory* worthy of the name. It is an analytical study of the matter and leads to a close *acquaintance* with it. When applied to experience, in our case to the history of war, it leads to *familiarity* with the subject. The closer it comes to achieving this goal, the more it moves from being an objective form of knowledge to being the subjective form of a skill; it proves to be all the more effective where the nature of the matter allows no other resolution but by talent, becoming, in effect, an active element of talent itself.

When theory is applied to the phenomena that constitute war, it draws a clearer distinction among what, at first glance, seems to run together indiscriminately. Theory explains in detail the properties of the means used, pointing out the probable effects of those means and clearly defining the intended goals. It casts light on an in-depth, critical study of warfare. When it does so, it has achieved its primary goal. It then serves as a guide to anyone wishing to familiarize himself with war from books; it sheds light on his path at every turn, making his steps easier, informing his judgment, and protecting him from being led astray.

Theory is there to ensure that each person does not have to start from scratch and work his way through a subject, but finds the matter sufficiently ordered and explained. Theory should educate the mind of the future commander, or rather guide him in his process of self-education, but it should not accompany him on the battle-field, just as a wise teacher steers and facilitates the mental development of a youth without guiding him by the hand for the rest of his life. (H&P 141; H 290–291)

THE TRINITY OF WAR

War is not merely a true chameleon, since it changes its nature slightly in each particular instance. It is also a wondrous trinity when considered as a whole and in relation to its predominant tendencies, composed of the inherent violence of its fundamental nature, the hatred and enmity that must be considered as a blind natural instinct; of the interplay of probability and chance in war that give the mind room to act freely; and of the subordinate nature of a political instrument, making it subject to pure reason.

The first of these aspects relates more to the people, while the second relates more to the commander and his army; the third is the concern of the government. The passions that are to flare up in war must already be present in the people. The scope that the interplay of courage and talent will attain in the realm of probability and chance depends on the particular nature of the commander and the army, but the political goals are a matter for the government alone.

These three tendencies, which appear as three different sets of legislation, are deeply rooted in the nature of the subject, and yet variable in importance. Any theory that fails to consider one of them, or that attempts to establish some arbitrary relationship among them, would immediately conflict with reality to such an extent that it would have to be deemed worthless for that reason alone. (H&P 89, H 212–213)

Rationalism and Romanticism in *On War*

The formulation of the trinity is a superb illustration of the openness and independence in Clausewitz's thinking and his ability to synthesize the contrary trends of rationalism (reason) and romanticism (instinct and imagination) that prevailed in Europe.

Michael Handel, a contemporary expert on strategic theory, expresses similar thoughts in *Introduction to Clausewitz and Modern Strategy.*

> Another explanation for the timelessness of Clausewitz' analytical method is to be found in the equal weight he gave to both the rational and non-rational elements in the study of war. Like so many other German intellectuals of his time, he combined the best of two worlds—the tradition of the Enlightenment, which emphasized rational objective analysis and the search of clarity, with the German romantic tradition (formulated in part as a reaction to the French as representative of the Enlightenment), which focused on the psychological, emotional, intuitive, and subjective dimensions in the interpretation of the surrounding world. The dialectical relationship between the Enlightenment on the one hand and German romanticism on the other—the two elements complementing rather than contradicting one another— created synthesis on a higher level. Representing the duality of human nature, his theory is as successful in presenting the calculating and rational side of war as in analyzing its non-rational and unpredictable qualities. While war is waged primarily to achieve rational ends, it is not a rational process. Hence, his emphasis on the role of uncertainty, chance, friction, and luck in war owes as much to German romantic perceptions of the human condition as to Newtonian rationality.

THE THEATER OF STRATEGY

In which the author fearlessly extricates the essence of strategy
from the clutter of countless other factors.
He leads the reader to acknowledge that
those who wish to enter onto the theater of strategy
must abandon all hope
of finding the certainties and control to which
they are accustomed in other pursuits
and consider the surrender of such hopes as
a rite of passage in strategy.

The Clash of Wills

War is not part of the realm of the arts and sciences. Rather, it belongs to the realm of social existence. It is a conflict of great interests that is resolved in a bloody manner, and it is only in this respect that it differs from other conflicts. Instead of comparing war to art, it is more appropriately compared to trade, which is also a conflict of human interests and activities. Politics, which in turn may also be viewed as a sort of trade on a larger scale, is even closer to it. (H&P 149; H 303)

The essential difference is that war is not an act of the will aimed at inanimate matter, as it is in the mechanical arts, or against a living yet passive and yielding object, as in the case of the human mind and feelings in the fine arts. Rather, war is an act of the will aimed at a living entity that *reacts*.

How ill suited the patterns of thought that apply within the arts and sciences are to such activity is readily apparent. At the same time, it is easy to see how this constant searching and striving for laws similar to those that can be derived from the realm of inani-

Strife and Origination

It should be known that war is universal, that strife is justice, and all things come into existence by strife and necessity.

—Heraclitus (c. 540–480 B.C.)

René Thom, the French mathematician and recipient of the Field Medal, the most distinguished award in mathematics, is known as one of the founders of catastrophe theory. In his fundamental work on the behavior of dynamic systems in the real world, *Structural Stability and Morphogenesis,* he often invokes the earliest Western philosophers, whose teachings still bear the marks of the dualistic concepts of more ancient Eastern schools of thought. In drawing philosophical conclusions from his work he states:

Of course this requires the abandonment of a universal mechanism and Laplacian absolute determinism, but have these ever been anything but wishful thinking?

Our models attribute all morphogenesis to conflict, a struggle between two or more attractors. This is the 2,500 year old idea of the first pre-Socratic philosophers, Anaximander and Heraclitus. They have been accused of primitive confusionism [*sic*] because they used a vocabulary with human and social origins (conflict, injustice, etc.) to explain the apperance of the physical world, but I think they were far from wrong because they had the following fundamentally valid intuition: *the dynamical situations governing the evolution of natural phenomena are basically the same as those governing the evolution of man and societies.* [The italics are Thom's.]

Like some of Clausewitz's well-known maxims, this famous aphorism of Heraclitus has been abused or misinterpreted as a vindication of war and violence. Yet when applied to our modern notions of the economy, what they are saying is hardly contestable. In essence, they merely argue

> that for anything new to emerge, for progress to occur and new wealth to be created, there must exist an indeterminancy of events that gives room to free will and imagination, and that nothing short of a clash of forces— be they military, physical, or competitive—can yield this rich substrate of indeterminacy.

mate objects would necessarily lead to compounded errors. (H&P 149; H 303)

War is an act of force, and there are no limitations to the application of that force. Each party goads the other on, triggering an interaction that must, theoretically, lead to extremes. (H&P 77; H 194)

Therefore, if we are to use military action to force the enemy to do our bidding, we must either render him truly defenseless, or put him in a position where he is effectively threatened with that outcome. Consequently, disarming or defeating the enemy must always be the goal of military action.

War, however, is not the action of a living force upon a dead mass, since absolute passivity would not constitute war at all; rather, war is always a clash between two living forces. What we have said here concerning the ultimate goal of military action, therefore, must be assumed on both sides. Here again, there is interaction. As long as I have failed to defeat my enemy, I must fear that he will defeat me; therefore, I am not in sole control; he controls me just as I control him. (H&P 77; H 194–195)

If we wish to defeat the enemy, we must gauge our efforts against his power of resistance. That power is the product of two inseparable factors, to wit: the *scope of the means available to him* and the *strength of his will.*

The scope of the available means can be calculated, since it is based on numbers, but the strength of the enemy's will is far more difficult to measure, and can be estimated only in relation to the strength of his underlying motivation. Assuming that we can obtain a fair estimate of his probable power of resistance, we can gauge our efforts accordingly—increasing them so that they carry the day or, if our means are insufficient to do so, making our efforts as great as possible. However, our enemy is doing the same thing, leading to yet another escalation that, in pure theory, must again result in striving for extremes. (H&P 77; H 195)

Friction

In war, everything is very simple, but the simplest thing is difficult. Someone who has no personal experience of war does not understand where the difficulties that are constantly discussed actually lie, nor the reasons for the brilliance and exceptional mental ability the commander must possess. Everything seems so simple; all the necessary knowledge seems so obvious, and all the deductive reasoning so insignificant that, by comparison, the simplest task of higher mathematics impresses us with a certain degree of scientific dignity. If one has experienced war, however, all these things become understandable, yet it remains extremely difficult to describe the invisible yet ubiquitous factor that causes this change.

Consider the example of a traveler who decides, late in the afternoon, to cover two more stages before dark, another four or five hours on a paved road, with a change of horse at each stage: nothing to it. But when he reaches the next stage, he finds that there are no horses, or only poor ones; the terrain is hilly, the road in disrepair. The night grows dark, and he is glad to find even meager accommodations when he reaches the next stage after this arduous journey.

Similarly in war, countless minor events—the sorts of things that can never be properly taken into account on paper—conspire to decrease efficiency, and one always falls far short of the goal. These difficulties happen over and over again, and cause a sort of friction that only those who have experienced war can accurately understand.

Negative Capability

Poet John Keats may have been talking about a quality that a literary "man of achievement" must have, but his description of "Negative Capability" bears considerable resemblance to the needs of military genius confronted with friction in war.

Keats, in a famous letter to his brothers (December 21, 1817), tells us that when returning from a party with friends he had:

> not a dispute but a disquisition with Dilke, on various subjects; several things dovetailed in my mind, & at once it struck me, what quality went to form a Man of Achievement especially in Literature & which Shakespeare possessed so enormously—I mean Negative Capability, that is when man is capable of being in uncertainties, Mysteries, doubts, without any irritable reaching after fact & reason. . . .

Negative Capability is being at ease when in bafflement or doubt and not seeking escapes at any cost. Clausewitz would agree that a commander must possess this faculty. Keats, as a man of letters, does not extend his image to the action one should take while in this state. Clausewitz, being a man of action, goes beyond Keats to assert that decisions to act benefit far more from the full consciousness of one's doubts than from illusory attempts to dispel those doubts. Doubts pushed aside will exact revenge; doubts properly entertained can be made to serve as scaffolding for thoughtful action.

Friction is the concept that best approximates the distinction between real war and war on paper. (H&P 119; H 261–262)

The military machine—the army and everything that goes with it—is basically very simple, which makes it seem easy to manage. But we must remember that no part of it consists of a single piece, that everything is made up of individuals, each of whom still has his own friction at every turn. In theory, it sounds quite good: The battalion leader is responsible for carrying out the order that has been given, and since the battalion has been formed into a cohesive unit through discipline, and the leader is a man of established devotion to duty, the beam pivots on its iron pin with minimal friction. But that is not how things are in the real world, and war immediately reveals everything that is excessive and untrue in a theory. The battalion is always made up of a number of men, the least significant of whom may very well bring things to a halt or cause things to go awry. The dangers that war entails, the physical efforts it requires, intensify this misfortune to such an extent that they must be deemed its most considerable cause.

Therefore, this terrible friction, which is not concentrated in just a few points as it is in mechanics, is everywhere in contact with chance, with consequences that are impossible to calculate, for the very reason that they are largely elements of chance. (H&P 119–120; H 262)

Awareness of this friction is a major component of the often-admired experience of warfare that is required of a good general. Obviously, the best general is not necessarily the person with the greatest awareness of this friction, and on whom it makes the greatest impression (this produces a class of anxious generals of a sort commonly found among those with experience). Rather, the general must have knowledge of friction in order to overcome it, where possible, and in order not to expect a level of precision in his operations that simply cannot be achieved owing to this very friction. (H&P 120; H 263)

Friction and Entropy

In 1775, the French Academy of Sciences formally ruled to disregard all purported inventions of perpetual motion machines. In 1850 Rudolf Clausius, a professor of physics at the Artillery and Engineering School in Berlin, proposed the Second Law of Thermodynamics and introduced the concept of entropy.

These dates bracket not only Clausewitz's life (1780–1831), but also a period of brilliant scientific activity, during which the notion of friction advanced from a long recognized but little understood nuisance in mechanical engineering to an acknowledged manifestation of several fundamental properties of matter.

Perpetual motion machines are now known to violate one or more of the laws of thermodynamics, but not until 1920 did Walther Hermann Nernst (also working in Berlin) elaborate the third law of thermodynamics and thereby reveal that entropy, and by implication, friction, were physical necessities, both unavoidable and ubiquitous.

Clausewitz was keenly interested in and aware of the scientific achievements of his day, and he must have been delighted to encounter in the emerging understanding of friction a term wonderfully suited for describing the unrelenting process of decay in all that humanity carefully orders. There is little doubt that had he written *On War* after 1850, he would have made good use of the term *entropy*.

Ironically, the notion of inevitable confusion and decay may be integral to military affairs in particular—after all, Edward Murphy was working as an engineer for the U.S. Air Force when, in the 1940s, he offered his famous restatement of entropy in human affairs: If anything can go wrong, it will.

Yet, in spite of all the evidence from science and folk wisdom that supports the notion and ubiquity of friction, the insight is most commonly honored in the breach. Planning is a necessity in any organized activity of some complexity. To assume, at the same time, that carefully laid out plans may not have much validity is psychologically hard and to suggest the same to an organization at large, whose adherence to plans is essential, is positively self-defeating. The illusion, however, that somehow by redoubling one's efforts in analyzing the contingencies of the future, one can reduce friction to a negligible quantity is more pernicious still. To the contrary, the greater the effort and sophistication applied to plans, the more likely that they succumb to friction.

It may be more useful to think of friction as a goblin, or more accurately as an entire army of them, more mischievious than malicious, more humorous than cynical, and with an irrepressible appetite for sabotaging the more elaborate plans and those who put faith in them. They are not good news, to be sure, but they are impartial between conflicting parties (unless tempted by one more than by the other). To those who do not defy them by denial, they create as much in new opportunities as they have wrecked in careful calculation. Strategists, in particular, are well advised to entertain a healthy working relationship with them.

Therefore friction, as we refer to it here, is what makes the seemingly easy so difficult. (H&P 121; H 264)

All matters of war pertain only to what is probable and not to sure outcomes. In all cases, what is lacking in certainty must be left to chance or fate. Obviously, we can insist on leaving as little to chance as possible, but only in a specific instance—in other words, *as little as is possible in that particular case.* It is not true that we should always choose the case with the least uncertainty. That would be a terrible mistake, as all of our theoretical deliberations show. There are instances in which the most daring course of action is the wisest choice.

Now whenever the actor leaves something to chance, his personal merit, and thus his responsibility, would no longer seem to be at stake. Nevertheless, we cannot resist feeling an inward sense of satisfaction when our hopes are met, and a sense of dissatisfaction when they are dashed. *But we should not take this any further and try to derive a judgment of right or wrong from the mere outcome, or, rather, what we make of the outcome.*

Knightean Uncertainty

American economist Frank H. Knight (1885–1972), who is considered to be among the most influential economic thinkers of the twentieth century and is a founder of the Chicago School of Economics, broke new ground by distinguishing between risk, where outcomes can be identified and their probabilities gauged, and uncertainty proper, where outcomes and their probabilities elude analysis. Risk can be insured; uncertainty cannot. In his seminal work, *Risk, Uncertainty, and Profit* (Boston: Riverside Press, 1921), he attributed entrepreneurial profit to successful engagement with uncertainty proper.

Michael Handel, in a discussion of probability in Clausewitz, expresses Knightean uncertainty.

Yet in no work other than *On War* are the roles of uncertainty, chance, friction, risk, and other related concepts brought into such a clear focus. Other than the primacy of politics, chance and uncertainty are the concepts most crucial for an understanding of Clausewitz' theory on war. These are the concepts that led him from the abstract level of theory and the ideal type of war to the ambiguous realities of war. This view of war as activity in which even the true probabilities are unknown must have been the central element in his decision not to write a scientific study of the subject.

But we cannot deny that the pleasure the mind experiences when our hopes are fulfilled and our displeasure when they are not draw upon a feeling lurking deep within. We like to think that there is a fine thread, undetectable by the mind, linking the outcome attributed to chance and the genius of the actor. Lending credence to this analysis is the fact that our personal interest increases, to the point of becoming a definite emotion, when that individual repeatedly experiences success or failure. This should convince us that luck in war is of a far nobler nature than luck in a game. We take pleasure in following the career of a soldier who has not in some way done us injury. (H&P 167; H 330)

THE FOG OF UNCERTAINTY

By the word *intelligence* we mean all the information we have about the enemy and his country, that is, the basis for our own plans and actions. If we consider for a moment the nature of this information, how unreliable and variable it is, we soon get a feel for how dangerous the edifice of war is, and how easily it can collapse, burying us under its rubble. All the books say that only accurate information should be relied upon, and that we must always be suspicious, yet this is nothing but wretched book learning. This is the sort of wisdom the writers of systems and compendia resort to when they have nothing better to add.

Much of the intelligence that we receive in war is contradictory, even more of it is plain wrong, and most of it is fairly dubious. What one can require of an officer, under these circumstances, is a certain degree of discrimination, which can only be gained from knowledge of men and affairs and from good judgment. The law of probability must be his guide. This difficulty is significant enough when preparing plans in an office while still outside the actual theater of war; but it is infinitely greater in the tumult of war with the reports coming in thick and fast. Still, it is fortunate if these reports, by contradicting each other, create a sort of balance that invites a critical review. The situation is much worse for an untested commander if chance fails to perform this service for him, but instead each report supports the last, confirming and expanding upon it, painting the picture in new colors, until we are forced to come to a hasty decision. Soon, though, the decision is recognized as a misstep, and all the reports are unmasked as lies, exaggerations, errors, and so forth. In short, most information is wrong, and men's fears become a driving force for lies and inaccuracies. As a rule, most men believe bad news before good, and tend to exaggerate the bad news somewhat. Though they may subside as quickly as the ocean waves, the dangers reported in this way, like the waves, keep coming back without clear reason. The commander must stand as firm in his inner convictions as the rock against which the waves pound. This is not an easy task; anyone who does not have a naturally buoyant character or who has not trained and improved his judgment through the experience of war should adopt a rule of acting against his own inner convictions, forcing himself to incline toward his hopes and away from his fears. Only in this way can he maintain the proper sense of balance. (H&P 117; H 258–259)

This difficulty of *seeing things correctly,* which is one of war's greatest frictions, causes things to appear quite differently from what one had initially thought. The impressions left by deliberate calculations are far less vivid than those of the senses, to the extent that there probably has never yet been a single significant undertaking where the commander did not have to overcome fresh doubts at the outset of the action. Ordinary men therefore, who follow the inspiration of others, become uncertain on the field of action. They believe that they have found circumstances to be different from what they expected, and all the more so because, here again, they follow the lead of others. But even a man who makes his own plans and now sees things for himself easily loses confidence in his former opinions. Deep confidence in himself must protect him against the pressure of the moment. Once the stage settings that fate erects in the theater of war are cleared away, bearing thickly applied images of danger, and once the horizons are expanded, his former convictions will be confirmed in the course of events. This is one of the great rifts between *planning* and *execution.* (H&P 117–118; H 259–260)

DANGER IN WAR

Now we step into the battle raging before us, still almost like a theater scene, to the nearest division commander. Here one shot follows close on the last, and the noise of our own guns adds to the din. From the division commander onward to the brigadier, a man of recognized bravery, carefully positioned behind a hill, a house, or some trees—a sure sign of increasing danger. Grapeshot clatters on rooftops and in the fields, cannon balls roar by and over us in all directions; another step toward the troops, toward the infantry that has remained at their posts with indescribable steadfastness through-out hours of this firefight. The air here is filled with whistling shot, announcing their nearness by the short, sharp noise as they fly past within inches of our ears, our heads, and our hearts. In addition to all this, compassion at the sight of those mutilated and fallen fills our pounding hearts with pity.

The novice cannot proceed through these various layers of increasing danger without sensing that the light of reason moves here through a different medium, and refracts differently than in the realm of speculative thought. Indeed, it would take quite an extraordinary man not to lose the ability to make an immediate decision during these first impressions. True, habit soon dulls these impressions considerably; within half an hour, we begin to treat everything in our surroundings more indifferently, some more quickly than others. But an ordinary person never quite achieves impartiality and his natural mental elasticity. We see, here again, that ordinary qualities are insufficient, and this is all the more true the greater the sphere of activity to be fulfilled. Enthusiastic, stoic, innate bravery and domineering ambition, as well as long experi-ence with danger—all this must be present if all the actions under-taken in these difficult circumstances are not to fall short of the mark that, in the study, may seem quite ordinary.

Friction and Learning

In disruptive situations, action must be taken before careful plans are made. Because much less can be known about what markets need or how large they can become, plans must serve a very different purpose: They must be plans for learning rather than plans for implementation. By approaching a disruptive business with the mindset that they can't know where the market is, managers would identify what critical information about new markets is most necessary and in what sequence that information is needed. Project and business plans would mirror those priorities, so that key pieces of information would be created, or important uncertainties resolved, before expensive commitments of capital, time, and money were required.

Clayton M. Christensen, in *The Innovator's Dilemma* (1997), addresses the effect of dramatically innovative technologies on established businesses. In such situations, the fog of business is at its thickest and friction reigns supreme. In a spirit that Clausewitz would have recognized, Christensen warns against the sort of planning that pretends there is no fog out there.

Danger is a part of war's friction, and a proper conception of that danger is necessary for a true understanding of war. That is why I have mentioned it here. (H&P 113–114; H 254–255)

THINKING STRATEGY

*In which the concrete problems of strategy enter the center stage
and the author furnishes practical demonstration that
strategy will thrive on thinking
if one lets thinking benefit from strategy in equal measure.*

*The fresh breeze of dialectics
rips away the cobwebs of doctrine
that have obscured the boundary between theory
and practical judgment
at which sound theory should halt
and let the practitioner proceed.*

Tactics and Strategy

The conduct of war is the planning and conduct of combat. Were this combat a single act, there would be no need for further subdivision. But combat consists of a greater or lesser number of *individual acts, each complete in itself,* which we call *engagements,* which constitute new things. This gives rise to an entirely different activity, namely, *individually planning and conducting* these engagements and *joining them together* to achieve the objective of the war. The first is called *tactics,* the second, *strategy.*

This division into tactics and strategy is now quite commonplace in practice, and everyone is reasonably certain where to categorize a particular factor without necessarily being aware of the reasons underlying that classification. Where such categories are used blindly, however, there must be a deeply rooted reason behind it. We have searched for that reason, and we can say that it is, in fact, this common usage that led us to it. On the other hand, we cannot accept the arbitrary and irrelevant definitions of the concept that some authors have sought, for the very reason that they are not established in common usage.

According to our classification, therefore, tactics teaches the *use of armed forces in engagements,* while strategy teaches the *use of engagements to achieve the objectives of the war.*

How the concept of the individual or independent engagement is more narrowly defined, and the conditions to which that entity is subject, cannot be clearly delineated until we examine the engagement in closer detail. At this point, we must be content to state that in terms of space, in relation to simultaneous battles, the unity extends only as far as the personal command, but in terms of time, that is, in successive engagements, it extends until the crisis that marks every engagement has been passed. (H&P 128; H 270–271)

If we do not learn to treat war and its individual campaigns as a chain made up of individual engagements, each always leading to the next, and if we espouse the notion that the capture of particular

---

Cornwallis in Carolina

A classic example of misjudging the relative value of the engagement and the campaign—of tactical and strategic dimensions—is the British campaign in the Carolinas during the American Revolution. In 1780 and 1781, the British object was to conquer the American South, which the British thought was less sympathetic to the rebel cause than the North. In every engagement, the main British army under General Charles Cornwallis drove its American opponents from the field.

In the process of each tactical victory, however, Cornwallis continued to suffer casualties and only deepened his logistical problems. After his last victory, at Guilford Courthouse, Cornwallis discovered that he had lost the capacity to hold Georgia and the Carolinas. The scattered garrisons he had left to hold the conquered territory were picked off by the Americans one by one. He withdrew into Virginia, where he was trapped between Washington's army and the French navy at Yorktown. His defeat there marked the de facto end of the war.

geographic points and the occupation of undefended provinces is *something worthwhile in itself,* then we are likely to consider them as incidental advantages. If we look at it that way, and not as a link within the whole series of events, we fail to ask whether this possession might lead to greater disadvantages down the line. How often we find this mistake made in military history!

We might put it this way: Just as a merchant cannot separate out and save the profit from one single transaction, in war a single advantage cannot be separated from the success of the whole undertaking. Just as the merchant must always operate with the sum of all his assets, in war it is only the final total that decides whether an individual item is an advantage or disadvantage. (H&P 182; H 353)

Tactics deals with the form of the individual engagement, while strategy deals with its use. Both affect the conditions of marches, encampments, and billets through the engagement only, items that become tactical or strategic depending on whether they relate to the form or the significance of the engagement.

Of course, many readers will consider this careful distinction between two so closely related concepts as tactics and strategy to be pointless, because it does not have an immediate influence on the conduct of war itself. One would, of course, have to be an absolute pedant to expect to see the immediate effects of a theoretical distinction played out on the battlefield.

The first task of any theory is to clarify terms and concepts that are confused and, one might even say, have become thoroughly entangled. Only after agreement has been reached regarding terms and concepts can we hope to consider the issues easily and clearly, and expect to share the same viewpoint with the reader. Tactics and strategy are activities that pervade each other in space and time, but they remain essentially different; their internal laws and their relationship to each other simply cannot be clearly thought through without establishing the concepts involved in a precise manner. (H&P 132; H 277–278)

TACTICS INTERACTING WITH STRATEGY

At one time, battle was the whole of war, and it will always remain its principal part. However, the order of battle belongs much more to tactics than to strategy. Our only aim in discussing its derivation was to show how tactics, by organizing the whole into smaller units, paved the way for strategy.

The larger armies became, the more they were spread out across large distances, and the more diverse the interactions of the individual parts, the more room there was for strategy. Thus the order of battle as well, as understood in our definition, had to enter into a sort of reciprocal action with strategy, an interaction that is most clear at the end points where tactics and strategy meet, in other words, at those moments when the general deployment of military forces crosses over into specific plans for the engagement. (H&P 293; H 520)

In light of the ideas we have adopted with regard to tactics and strategy, it is obvious that a change in tactics will necessarily have an impact on strategy. If tactical phenomena in one instance are completely different from those in another, then strategic phenomena must differ as well if they are to remain logically consistent and rational. (H&P 226; H 420)

THE ADAPTABILITY OF STRATEGY

Strategy is the use of the engagement to achieve the objectives of the war; therefore, it must give an aim to the whole military action that corresponds to the goal of the war. Strategy, then, determines the plans for the individual campaigns, and orders the engagements within them. Because most of these things are based on assumptions that do not always materialize and on a number of other, more specific details that cannot be determined in advance, it follows that

A Freely Creative Activity

General Ludwig Beck (1880–1944) was a senior commander in the German army immediately prior to World War II. His writings—abounding with specific references to Clausewitz—show that he was a keen student of his predecessor, and that in particular he understood very well two crucial Clausewitzian concepts: first, the continuum of politics and war; and second, the value of critical strategic analysis at the highest level of military decisions. Beck was not afraid to act on his intellectual convictions; as chief of the General Staff from 1935 until his resignation in 1938, he opposed Hitler's initiation and conduct of the war and, in 1944, he was among the leaders of the failed attempt to assassinate Hitler, for which he paid with his life.

> Bringing together and arranging all the foundations for a possible war necessarily results in a need to prepare a plan of war. As self-evident as this need may seem, it still deserves particular attention. There is certainly great danger when plans are drawn up in preparation for and during war—the sphere of uncertainty where the independent will of the enemy, chance, and error play a major role. A hallmark of true commanders has always been their ability to act with sovereign independence in keeping with the circumstances, and to free themselves in a timely way from the shackles of a predetermined plan, however well crafted that plan may be. This is also why it is carefully stated in the introduction to our German regulation for the "Conduct of Troops" that: "The conduct of war is an art, a freely creative activity based on a scientific foundation."

strategy must be developed at the battle site itself. In this way, specifics can be formulated on the spot, and modifications, which never cease to be necessary, can be made to the entire plan. Thus, strategy can never turn its eyes away for even a moment.

This has not always been the view, at least with regard to the overall plan, as can be seen by the practice of formulating strategy within the cabinet and not in the field. That approach is permissible only when the cabinet is so close to the army that it serves as the army's main headquarters.

. . . A prince or a general who knows how to arrange his warfare strictly in accordance with his objective and means does neither too much nor too little, thereby giving the best possible proof of his genius. But the effects of this genius are evident not so much in new ways of acting, which would be immediately visible, as in the successful outcome of the entire undertaking. We should admire the exact fulfillment of tacit assumptions and the unobtrusive harmony of the action as a whole, which are expressed only in its overall success. (H&P 177–178; H 345–346)

Simple, but Not Easy

T he means and forms that strategy uses are so very simple and so familiar from their constant repetition that common sense must find it absurd to hear critics so often engaged in such pretentious discussion of it. In these discussions, even such a run-of-the-mill event as turning an opponent's flank is hailed as a stroke of absolute genius, the deepest of insights, even the most comprehensive wisdom. Could there possibly be anything triter anywhere in the world of ivory-towered theorists?

It is even more absurd when we consider that this same critical discussion generally excludes all moral quantities from theory, focusing solely on material aspects, so that everything can be reduced to a few mathematical formulas of balance and superiority, time and space, and a few angles and lines. If that were all it really amounted to, all this misery would barely constitute a science problem for a schoolboy.

But frankly, scientific formulas and problems are not at all the issue here. The relations of material objects are all very straightforward. It is more difficult to comprehend the intellectual forces that are involved. But even there, it is only at the highest levels of strategy that intellectual complications and a great diversity of factors and relations are to be found. It is here that strategy touches most closely upon politics and statesmanship, or rather becomes both itself; and it is here that, as we have said before, they have more influence on how much or how little is to be done than they have on how it is to be executed. Where execution is a predominant concern, as in the individual events of war—be they great or small—these intellectual factors are already reduced to a small number. (H&P 178; H 346–347)

So everything in strategy is very simple, but that does not make everything easy. Once it has been determined what a war is intended to do and can accomplish, it is easy to map out its course. But following that course unwaveringly, carrying out the plan and not being thrown off course thousands of times for a thousand reasons, requires great mental clarity and confidence, in addition to great strength of character. Of a thousand exceptional men, some of whom may be distinguished for their intellect, others for their good judgment, and still others for their daring or strength of will, perhaps not even one will possess all these characteristics, which would make him an above-average commander.

It sounds strange, but everyone familiar with war in this regard would agree that it takes much greater strength of will to make a key strategic decision than a tactical one. With tactics, the actor is swept along by the moment and feels caught up in a whirlwind so intense that to struggle against it would result in the direst of consequences. He suppresses his misgivings and forges ahead boldly. With strategy, where everything moves much more slowly, there is plenty of room for one's own misgivings, objections, and ideas— and those of others—and for inopportune remorse. With strategy, one does not see at least half the situation with one's own eyes; rather, everything must be guessed at and presumed, which decreases one's level of conviction. As a result, most generals become bogged down in ineffectual fears when they should be taking action. (H&P 178–179; H 347–348)

FREDERICK'S 1760 CAMPAIGN

Now let us have a glance at history. Consider the campaign of Frederick the Great in 1760, famous for its stunning marches and maneuvers, a true masterpiece of strategy in the eyes of the critics. Are we, then, to be beside ourselves with admiration that the king first wanted to turn Daun's right flank, and then his left, and again his right? Are we to see in this some deep wisdom? No, we cannot, if we wish to judge naturally and without pretentiousness. Rather, we must first and foremost wonder at the king's wisdom: Pursuing a significant objective with limited forces, he did not attempt anything that lay beyond the grasp of those forces, but *exactly enough* to achieve his objective. His wisdom is clear not only in this campaign, but in all three wars that the great king fought. . . .

Marches intended for turning a flank to the right or left are easily planned. The idea of keeping a small force close together so that it can meet a scattered enemy on equal terms at any point, and of multiplying that force through rapid movement, is as easily conceived as expressed. So this discovery cannot arouse our admiration; all we can confess regarding such simple things is that they are, indeed, simple.

But just let a commander try to imitate Frederick the Great in these matters. Many years afterward, writers of eyewitness accounts were still commenting on the risk, indeed the rashness, of the king's encampments, and we can be sure that the risk appeared three times as great at the time he took it as it did thereafter.

The same was true of the marches that took place under the eyes, often under the cannons, of the enemy army. Frederick the Great took up these encampments and undertook these marches because Daun's methods, his manner of drawing up his army, his sense of responsibility, and his character persuaded him that his encampments and marches were risky, but not ill considered. But it required the king's boldness, determination, and strength of will to

Frederick the Great

Frederick was badly outnumbered throughout the Seven Years' War (1756 to 1763), in which emergent Prussia was pitted against France, Russia, and the Habsburg Empire. Although Prussia was allied to Britain, which provided substantial funding and some military assistance (the King of England was also King of Hanover, a fairly large German state), England's real interests were overseas and Frederick was largely on his own. Although his natural tendency was to seek decisive victory in battle, he knew that he could never militarily overwhelm his larger and wealthier opponents; no matter how many victories he won, there was always another enemy army to worry about. Therefore, he sought to exhaust his enemies financially and psychologically by prolonging the war.

This required him to avoid decisive engagements unless he had reason to believe he could inflict disproportionate casualties.

Frederick's achievement is all the greater in that his chief opponent, the Austrian Field Marshal, Count Leopold Joseph Daun, was himself, despite Clausewitz's repeated disparagement, a very capable soldier who defeated Frederick in battle a number of times.

Clausewitz's point in this discussion is that Frederick is to be admired not only for his strategy, which was indeed simple, though not easy, but also for the skill and determination with which he executed it. This is an illustration of *military genius,* which is no more a matter of character and personality than of intellect.

view matters in this light, and not to be shaken and intimidated by the risk that was still being spoken and written about 30 years after the fact. In such a situation, few commanders would have believed that this simple expedient of strategy would be workable. (H&P 179–180; H 348–349)

Attack and Defense

Whenever two concepts form a true logical antithesis, in other words, one is the complement of the other, the one is essentially implied in the other. However, if the limitations of our mind do not allow us to consider both at once, and to find the totality of one by mere antithesis in the totality of the other, in any case, nevertheless, strong light is shed by one that is adequate to illuminate many parts of the other.

Hence, in addressing the attack, we shall most often have the same subjects before us [as] when considering the defense. However, it is not our view, and not in the nature of the subject, to proceed in the manner of so many engineering textbooks by circumventing, or demolishing, everything we established in terms of the defense, or proving that there is an infallible method of attack for every means of defense. The defense has its own strengths and weaknesses. If the strengths are not insurmountable, their cost may be disproportionate. This must remain true from every point of view, or else we shall be contradicting ourselves. Moreover, it is not our intent to make an exhaustive study of the reciprocal action of the various means. Every means of defense leads to a means of attack, but this is often so patently obvious that there is no need to make the transition from the standpoint of defense to that of the attack to become aware of it. One automatically leads to the other. Our intent is to indicate, for each subject, what the special features of the attack are to the extent that they do not proceed directly from the defense. (H&P 523; H 869–870)

ATTACK AND DEFENSE IN TACTICS

First we must examine the circumstances that lead to victory in an engagement. It seems to us that only three things provide critical advantages: *surprise,* the *advantage of terrain,* and *attack from several sides.*

Surprise is effective if one moves against the enemy at a particular point using far more troops than he expected. This numerical superiority is quite different from such superiority in general; it is the most powerful agent in the art of war. How the advantage of terrain contributes to victory is fairly self-evident; the only point to consider is that it is not merely an issue of obstacles that the attacker encounters during his advance, such as steep slopes, high mountains, marshy streams, hedges, and so on, but it is also an advantage of terrain if these things give us the opportunity to deploy our troops on the terrain in a concealed manner. Even on unremarkable terrain, those familiar with it can be said to have a certain advantage. The attack from several sides includes all tactical circumventions, large and small, and its effectiveness is based in part on the doubled effectiveness of the firearms, and in part on the fear of being cut off.

How, then, do the attack and defense relate in terms of these concerns?

Taking into consideration the three principles of victory just presented, it becomes clear that the attacker has only a small part of the first and last principles in his favor, while the greater part, and the second principle, are available only to the defender.

The only advantage the attacker has is the actual surprise attack of his full force, whereas the defender is capable of creating constant surprise during the engagement by the strength and form of his attacks. (H&P 360; H 618–619)

ATTACK AND DEFENSE IN STRATEGY

First, we must ask: What are the circumstances that yield success in strategy?

There is no victory in strategy, as has been stated. Strategic success, on the one hand, is the beneficial preparation for tactical victory. The greater the strategic success, the more certain is the victory in the engagement. On the other hand, strategic success lies in using the hard-won victory. The more events that strategy, through its combinations, can take advantage of in the aftermath of a successful engagement, the more it can snatch from the collapsing ruins whose foundations have been shaken by the fighting, and the more it can gather in sweeping motions what, in the battle itself, had to be taken individually and with great effort, the greater the success.

The factors that favor or facilitate this success—in other words, the main principles of strategic effectiveness—are as follows: (1) the advantage of terrain; (2) surprise, either in the form of an actual sudden attack, or through an unexpected deployment of greater force at particular points; (3) attack from several sides, all three as in tactics; (4) aid to the theater of war by means of fortifications and everything relating to them; (5) the assistance of the people; and (6) the use of great moral forces.

How, then, do attack and defense relate in terms of these concerns?

The defender has the advantage of terrain, the attacker that of surprise. This is the same for strategy as for tactics. However, it must be noted that in strategy, the surprise attack is an infinitely more effective and important means than it is in tactics. In tactics, a surprise attack can rarely be expanded to achieve a great victory, whereas in strategy, a surprise attack has quite often put an end to the entire war. However, we must note once more that the use of this device is predicated on major, crucial, and rare errors by the opponent. Therefore it does not tip the scales much in favor of the attack. (H&P 363–364; H 622–623)

THE DYNAMICS OF DEFENSE

What is the concept of defense? The fending off of a blow. What, then, is its characteristic feature? Waiting for the blow. This characteristic makes any action a defensive one, and it is through this characteristic alone that defense can be distinguished from attack in war. However, since an absolute defense completely contradicts the concept of war, since only one party would then be waging war, defense in war can only be relative, and this characteristic must, therefore, be applied only to the concept as a whole, and must not be extended to all of its parts. A partial engagement is defensive if we wait for the onslaught, the charge of the enemy; an engagement is defensive if we await the attack, that is, the appearance of the enemy in front of our position, in our range of fire; a campaign is defensive if we wait for the enemy to enter our theater of war.

Characteristic features shared by all these cases are awaiting and fending off the enemy, which do not contradict the concept of war. That is because we may find it advantageous to wait for the charge against our bayonets, and the attack on our position and theater of war. Since we must return the enemy's blows if we ourselves are to wage war, however, this attacking action in a defensive war, in a certain sense falls under the heading of defense, that is, the offensive action that we take falls within the concept of position, or theater of war. Therefore, in a defensive campaign, we can fight offensively and use our individual divisions for attack in a defensive battle; lastly, even when we take up a defensive position against the enemy's onslaught, we still send bullets on the attack against him. The defensive form of the conduct of war, then, is not an instantaneous shield, but a shield formed by skillful blows. (H&P 357; H 613–614)

In tactics, every engagement, large or small, is a *defensive* engagement if we leave it up to the enemy to take the initiative and wait for him to appear on our front. From that point on, we can avail ourselves of all offensive means without losing the two advantages of defense previously specified, namely, that of waiting and that of terrain. In strategy, the campaign takes the place of the engagement, and the theater of war takes the place of terrain. Thereafter, however, the war overall takes the place of the campaign, and the entire country takes the place of the theater of war, and in both instances, the defense remains as it was in tactics.

The fact that defense is easier than the attack has already been noted generally, but since the defense has a negative purpose, that of *preserving,* and the attack has a positive one, that of *conquering,* and because conquering increases our own military resources while preserving does not, to express this point accurately we must say that the *defensive form of the conduct of war is inherently stronger than the attacking form.* This is the result we have been striving to achieve, because even though this is entirely natural and has been confirmed a thousand times over by experience, nonetheless it runs counter to prevailing opinion—proof of how concepts can become confused by superficial writers.

If defense is a stronger form of the conduct of war, but one with a negative purpose, it follows naturally that we must employ this form only for as long as we must, owing to our weak position. Likewise, we must abandon it as soon as we become strong enough to aim at the positive object. Now since we commonly obtain a better balance of strength when we are victorious through the defensive, it is also the natural progression in war to begin with the defense and end with the offensive. So it is just as contradictory with the concept of war to view defense as its ultimate purpose as it was to consider the passivity of defense as applying not only to the defense as a whole, but to each of its parts as well. In other words: A war in which we use victories merely to fend off attacks, without the intention of counterattacking, would be just as absurd as a battle in which the most absolute defense (passivity) governed every move. (H&P 358; H 614–615)

The Art of Defense: Waiting

[Previously] we noted that the absolute goal of a military action is in fact to overthrow the enemy when we believe that goal can be achieved. Now we should consider what remains to be done when the conditions are not ripe to achieve that goal.

These conditions presuppose a great physical or moral advantage or an immense spirit of enterprise, that is, an inclination to take great risks. When those factors are not present, a military action can have only two kinds of goal: either to seize a greater or lesser part of the enemy's territory or to hold onto one's own territory until a better moment comes along. This last goal is the more common one in a defensive war.

In determining which of these goals is the right one for us to pursue, we come back to the phrase used in the previous paragraph—holding off *until a better moment comes along.* With this approach, we expect the future to offer us better prospects; our decision to bide our time, that is, mount a defensive war, is always motivated by that view. Conversely, whenever we mount an offensive war, that is, make use of the present moment, we always expect the future to hold better prospects for the enemy's side than for our own. The third possibility, which is perhaps the most common one, is that neither side has any particular expectations for the future, and thus has no particular basis for making a decision. In this case, the offensive role clearly falls to the political aggressor, that is, the party that has a positive basis for action, since it took up arms to achieve that goal, and any time allowed to elapse without good reason is time lost. (H&P 601; H 984–985)

The concept of defense is fending off the attacker; waiting is part of this fending action, and we view this waiting both as the main characteristic of defense and as its main advantage.

Defense, then, is composed of two heterogeneous parts: waiting and acting. By relating the first to a specific object and thereby indicating that it must precede action, we have made it possible to combine the two into a single whole. But a defensive act, particularly a large action such as a campaign or an entire war, will not be composed of two large halves, in terms of time, the first being a time of waiting, and the second a time of pure action. Instead, it will be an interplay of these two states, so that waiting may run through the entire act of defense as a continuous thread.

We have attached such importance to waiting simply because the matter requires it. In earlier theories, admittedly, it was never brought up as a separate concept. In the real world, however, it has served continuously as a connecting thread, albeit often unconsciously. Waiting is such a fundamental part of the entire act of war that one scarcely seems possible without the other. Consequently, we shall have occasion to return to it often in what follows, since we will be pointing out its effects on the dynamic interplay of forces. (H&P 379; H 647–648)

The Art of Defense: Counterattacking

Even if the intent of war is merely to preserve the status quo, merely fending off a blow is contradictory to the concept of war, because the conduct of war is indisputably not merely passive. If the defender has achieved a significant advantage, the defense has done its work; under the protection of this advantage, the defender must return the blow, for otherwise he will be exposed to certain destruction. Wisdom dictates that we should strike while the iron is hot; we must use the superiority we have gained to ward off a second attack. How, when, and where this reaction is to take place is obviously subject to many other conditions. This transition to the counter-attack must be considered a natural tendency of defense, and thus a vital component of it. Whenever the victory achieved through the defensive form is not in some way used for gain in the military economy, whenever it withers away unused, so to speak, a serious mistake is being made.

A rapid, powerful transition to the attack—the glinting sword of vengeance—is the most brilliant moment of the defense. Anyone who does not think of it from the very beginning, or rather, anyone who does not include it within the concept of defense, will never understand the superiority of defense. He will always think only of the enemy's means that are destroyed or captured in the attack. But these means do not depend on how the knot is tied, but rather on how it is untied. Moreover, it is a rudimentary error to define the attack always as a sudden assault, and consequently to think of defense merely as desperation and confusion. (H&P 370; H 633–634)

THE ATTACK

Just as no defensive campaign is composed solely of defensive elements, no campaign of attack is composed solely of offensive elements. This is because, aside from the brief interim period that occurs in every campaign in which the two armies hold a defensive stance, every attack that does not lead to peace must necessarily end with a defense.

In this way, it is the defense itself that contributes to the weakening of the attack. This is much more than hairsplitting; rather, we consider it the greatest disadvantage of the attack that, after it is over, we are placed in an entirely disadvantageous defensive position. (H&P 572; H 943–944)

Lessons from Military Strategy

The Boston Consulting Group's founder, Bruce Henderson, observes that "many of the basic principles of strategy have been distilled from warfare." As examples, he cites a famous passage from Sun Tzu: "Supreme excellence consists in breaking the enemy's resistance with fighting. Thus the highest form of generalship is to baulk the enemy's plans; the next best is to prevent the junction of the enemy's forces; the next in order is to attack the enemy's army in the field; the worst policy of all is to besiege walled cities." Henderson also cites Napoleon: "The whole art of war consists in a well reasoned and extremely circumspect defensive, followed by a rapid and audacious attack."

Positional Advantage

In the section on defense, there is adequate discussion of the extent to which defensive positions force the enemy either to attack them or to give up his advance. Only those positions that do so are appropriate and suited to drain the attacking forces in whole or in part, or to neutralize them. To that extent, the attack can do nothing against them; in other words, there are no resources available to it to outweigh this advantage. However, not all defensive positions are like this. If the attacker sees that he can attain his objective without attacking them, it would be a mistake to mount an attack. If he cannot obtain his objective, then the question arises whether he can outmaneuver his opponent by threatening his flank.

Only if these means are ineffective will he decide to mount an attack against a good position, and attacking on the flank will always present somewhat fewer difficulties. The choice of which flank to attack, however, is determined by the position and direction of each side's lines of retreat, that is, the threat to the enemy's retreat and the security of one's own. Competition may arise between the two, and the advantage will go, naturally, to the first, since it is itself

STOCKHOLM

WEDEN

Baltic Sea

ST PETERSBURG

Volga

MOSCOW
✕ BORODINO

RIGA

TAUROGGEN

SMOLENSK

RUSSIA

KONIGSBERG

TILSIT

✕ FRIEDLAND

MINSK

✕ BEREZINA

Don

DANZIG

✕ EYLAU

PRUSSIA

BERLIN

GRAND DUCHY
OF
POLAND

WARSAW

Vistula

Oder

KIEV

Dnieper

DRESDEN
✕

PRAGUE

KRAKOW

TISBON

✕ AUSTERLITZ

CARPATHIANS

✕ WAGRAM

AUSTRIAN

VIENNA

PEST

BUDA

EMPIRE

Danube

BELGRADE

BUCHAREST

Danube

✕	BATTLES OF NAPOLEON
	AREA ADDED TO FRENCH EMPIRE OR INDIRECTLY RULED AFTER 1789
▢	FRENCH EMPIRE 1812
⋯	NATIONAL BORDERS 1812
⋯	CONFEDERATION OF THE RHINE BORDERS 1812

DALMATIA

Adriatic

Sea

OTTOMAN

CONSTANTINOPLE

Black Sea

KINGDOM
OF NAPLES

LES

SALONICA

EMPIRE

MESSINA

Aegean Sea

ATHENS

CILY

Attacking Strong Defenses

Torgau—November 1760 (Seven Years' War). Frederick attacked the Austrians under the capable Daun, who were in a very strong defensive position. After committing all of his reserves and near defeat, Frederick managed to drive the Austrians from the battlefield. However, his losses were very high and exceeded those of his enemy.

Wagram—July 1809. Napoleon had been defeated (his first defeat) by the Austrians under the skillful command of the Archduke Charles of Austria at the battle of Aspern-Essling in May. At Wagram, he defeated them and ended the war in his own favor, but, by some estimates at least, French losses in dead and wounded considerably exceeded the Austrians'.

Dresden—August 1813. Napoleon defeated the Austrian Field Marshal Karl Philipp, Prince of Schwarzenberg, inflicting disproportionately large casualties. Although Clausewitz is frequently negative about him, Schwarzenberg is generally well regarded. However, Clausewitz may be referring to the unusual command situation at the time: Schwarzenberg had the emperors of Russia and Austria, as well as the King of Prussia, in his camp.

Clausewitz's point in all this is that simply because there are a few examples of successful attacks made on well-entrenched and capable foes that is no reason to try it yourself. The probabilities are not in your favor.

---

offensive in nature and thus consistent with the attack, while the other is defensive in nature. This much is certain, however, and must be considered a fundamental truth: *It is dangerous to attack a capable enemy in a good position.* Examples of such battles in which the attack was successful abound, such as Torgau, Wagram (we exclude Dresden since the enemy, in that case, could not be characterized as capable). But overall, the number of such successes is small and pales in comparison to the number of instances in which we see the most resolute commanders opting not to act against good positions. (H&P 535; H 889–890)

Boldness and Confidence

Just as caution is the true genius of defense, boldness and confidence are the hallmarks of the attacker—not that the opposite qualities should be lacking in both, but that each of these qualities has greater affinity for one or the other. In fact, all these qualities are necessary only because action is not a mathematical construct, but an activity that takes place in the dark, or at most in faint light, in which we must trust the leader who is best suited to achieve our objective. The weaker the defender's morale, the more brazen the attack must be. (H&P 545; H 904)

Elements of Strategy

SUPERIORITY OF NUMBERS

Numerical superiority is the most common principle of victory in tactics as well as in strategy.

Strategy determines the place where, the time when, and the fighting forces with which the battle is to be fought. Owing to this threefold determination, strategy has extraordinary influence on the outcome of the battle. When tactics have completed the battle, and the result is in, whether victory or defeat, strategy uses the outcome in whatever way possible in accordance with the objective of the war. Naturally this objective is often quite distant.

Strategy determines the time, place, and force to be used, and can do so in various ways—each of which affects the outcome and the success of the battle differently.

If we then strip the battle of all modifications to which it may be subject owing to its purpose and the circumstances that lead up to it, and finally if we ignore the value of the troops, since that is a given quantity, what we have left is the unadorned concept of the engagement, that is, a formless battle distinguished only by the number of combatants. That number, then, is what will determine the victory. Simply from the number of abstractions that we have had to make to reach this point, it is clear that the superiority of numbers in an engagement is only one of the factors that make up a victory. Therefore, far from achieving everything, or even just the main thing, through superiority of numbers, we may actually have achieved very little, depending on what the contributing circumstances are.

But there are degrees of superiority. It may be twofold, threefold, fourfold, or more, and everyone understands that, in light of such an increase, superiority of numbers will necessarily overwhelm everything else.

In this regard, we must concede that superiority of numbers is the most important factor in the outcome of an engagement, but it must be large enough to offset all the other contributing circumstances. The immediate consequence is that we must focus the largest possible number of troops at the decisive point in the engagement.

The Battles of Leuthen and Rossbach

Battle of Rossbach—November 1757. Frederick, standing on the defense, surprised a combined Austrian and French army on the attack by changing his dispositions and pretending to retreat, while in fact setting up a large ambush. Frederick lost fewer than 1,000 men, the Austrians and French over 10,000.

Battle of Leuthen—December 1757. Frederick defeated the Austrians by an unorthodox maneuver, taking advantage of masking terrain to unexpectedly mass his attack on one wing of the superior enemy force. It is generally considered Frederick's masterpiece.

Whether or not these troops are sufficient, from this perspective we will have done everything that the means allowed. This is the first principle in strategy. (H&P 194–195; H 373–374)

At Leuthen, Frederick the Great defeated 80,000 Austrians with some 30,000 men, and at Rossbach, his 25,000 men beat 50,000 allies.

However, these are also the only examples of a victory won against an enemy with twice as many men, or more. We cannot justifiably cite the example of Charles XII, in the battle of Narva. At the time, the Russians were scarcely to be considered Europeans, and the main circumstances of the battle are not sufficiently known. At Dresden, Bonaparte had 120,000 against 220,000, not quite twice as many. At Kolin, Frederick the Great, with 30,000 men, was unable to defeat 50,000 Austrians, and similarly Bonaparte at the desperate battle at Leipzig had 160,000 men against 280,000, the superiority of numbers being far from twice as many.

All this may well indicate that in present-day Europe, it is very difficult even for the most talented general to achieve a victory against an enemy power that is twice as large. When we see that such double numbers weigh so heavily against the greatest of generals, we should not be the least bit surprised to find that in ordinary instances, in battles great and small, a significant superiority of numbers, one that need not exceed 2 to 1, is sufficient to grant victory regardless of how disadvantageous the other circumstances may be. One could, of course, imagine some situation in which having a tenfold superiority of numbers would still be insufficient; but in such cases, the term *engagement* hardly seems to apply. (H&P 195; H 375)

If we are truly convinced that everything possible can be achieved by force given significant superiority, then it is inevitable that this conviction will have an impact on our preparation for war, so that we take the field with as many troops as possible either to gain superiority ourselves, or to keep the enemy from doing so. So much for the absolute strength with which war should be waged.

The Battles of Narva, Dresden, Kolin, and Leipzig

Battle of Narva—November 20, 1700. Charles XII of Sweden, with about 8,000 men, practically wiped out a Russian army of about 40,000 during a blinding snowstorm. Clausewitz cites this battle as an odd example of a small force defeating one many times its size—but points out that the Russian army of the time (just before Peter the Great's westernizing reforms began to take hold) could not really be considered a modern Western army, whereas Charles's Swedish force was one of the best in Europe.

Dresden—late August 1813. Napoleon, under tremendous pressure from allied Russian, Prussian, and Austrian forces in the wake of his disaster in Russia the previous year, fought a series of brilliant battles in which he defeated numerically superior armies—though ultimately he was forced back into France and had to abdicate in 1814. At Dresden, an Austrian army caught part of Napoleon's force seemingly isolated and attacked with overwhelming numerical advantages. Napoleon arrived unexpectedly with reinforcements (total forces engaged: about 120,000 French against 220,000 allied troops) and stopped the Austrian advance. The following day, he concentrated his outnumbered army on one flank of the Austrians and drove them from the field. The Austrians took some 40,000 casualties, compared to 10,000 for the French. Almost immediately afterward, however, the same Austrian army inflicted a disastrous defeat on one of Napoleon's subordinates at the battle of Kulm when the emperor himself failed to appear—the French lost 17,000 out of 37,000 troops engaged, and the rest were scattered in flight. Clausewitz uses this battle (i.e., Dresden) to show that odds of 2 against 1 are about as much as even a genius like Napoleon could handle—assuming that both forces are modern Western armies.

Kolin—June 18, 1757. Frederick the Great was besieging Prague. An Austrian force of about 50,000 to 60,000 men moved to relieve the city. Trying to maintain the siege, Frederick took a part of his force—some 32,000 men—and attempted to drive the relieving army off. His attack was repulsed and he was forced to raise the siege and withdraw his entire army. Clausewitz uses this battle to demonstrate that even a genius of Frederick's calibre had a hard time coping with such odds—not quite 2 to 1 in this case—although Frederick also erred in trying to do too many things at once with limited forces.

Leipzig—October 16–19, 1813. Often called the Battle of the Nations, Leipzig represents the point at which the French nationalism of the revolutionary era was counterbalanced by the rival nationalisms France had stimulated through its earlier campaigns of conquest. Napoleon was driven into the city of Leipzig by converging Russian, Prussian, Austrian, and Swedish forces. German (Saxon) forces in the French army switched sides. Napoleon managed to escape with his army intact, but lost about 60,000 men and several hundred cannon. Again, Clausewitz highlights this battle to illustrate that not even the superb talent of Napoleon could overcome high odds—in this case about 4 to 7 against.

The scale of this absolute power will be determined by the government, and although the actual military activity begins with this determination, and although it is also a key strategic part of that military action, in most cases the general who is to lead these fighting forces in war must regard the absolute number of these troops as a given, whether because he had no part in determining their number or because circumstances prevented a sufficient number from being raised.

The only remaining course, therefore, is to create a relative superiority of numbers at the decisive point, if an absolute superiority cannot be achieved, by using the troops skillfully.

The most important factor in doing so, it seems, is to calculate the space and time. This has led people to consider that, in terms of strategy, the calculation of space and time covers nearly the entire subject of the use of fighting forces. Some have gone so far as to ascribe to great generals an internal organ specifically created for this purpose. (H&P 196; H 376–377)

Far more frequently, relative superiority, that is, the skillful direction of superior forces at the decisive point, is based on the correct assessment of this point and the appropriate direction that the forces receive right from the outset; in the determination needed to let the unimportant fall by the wayside in favor of what is important, that is, keeping one's forces united in an overwhelming mass, Frederick the Great and Bonaparte provide two typical examples.

In this way, we believe that we have returned to the superiority of numbers the significance it deserves. It must be considered the fundamental idea, always to be sought first, and to the greatest extent possible.

Conceiving of this superiority as a necessary condition for victory, however, would be a complete misunderstanding of our argument. Rather, the upshot of our reasoning is merely to point out the value that we must place on the numerical strength of the fighting forces in the engagement. If those numbers are kept as large as possible, the principle is served well enough, and only a view of all the circumstances together can determine whether the engagement should be avoided owing to a lack of numbers. (H&P 197–196; H 378)

In our day, armies are so similar to each other in weapons, equipment, and training that there are no significant differences between the best and worst of them in these matters. Education may still make a significant difference among the technical corps, but this generally means only that some invent and introduce better arrangements, and the others are quick to imitate them. Even generals of lesser rank, those who command corps and divisions, all apparently share the same outlook and methods. Consequently, aside from the talent of the commander in chief, which depends entirely on chance and hardly bears any constant relationship to the education of the people and of the army, familiarity with war is the only thing that can produce unambiguous superiority. The greater the equilibrium in all these matters, the more decisive the impact of relative strength. (H&P 282; H 504)

CONCENTRATION IN SPACE

The best strategy is *always to be very strong,* first in general, and then at the decisive point. Therefore, aside from the effort that creates the strength in forces, and that does not always originate with the general, there is no higher or simpler law for strategy than *keeping one's forces concentrated.* No troops should be separated from the main army unless an *urgent* purpose calls them away. We hold fast to this criterion, and consider it a reliable guide. We will gradually discover what the reasonable causes for separating the army may be. Then we will also see that this principle cannot have the same general consequences in every way, but rather, that they change depending on the purpose and the means.

It sounds unbelievable, and yet it has happened a hundred times over, that troops have been divided and separated merely according to some vague sense of how things are conventionally done, without a clear understanding of why it is being done.

If one recognizes the unification of all the fighting forces as the norm, and any separation or division as a deviation from that norm for which reasons must be provided, not only will that folly be avoided entirely, but many specious reasons for such separation will be ruled out. (H&P 204; H 388)

UNIFICATION IN TIME

If, in tactics, the commander cannot decide everything with the first success, he must fear the next moment. It follows, then, that for the success of the first moment he will use only the number of forces that seem necessary for that purpose, and that he will hold the remaining forces in reserve out of harm's way, beyond the range of firearms and away from hand-to-hand combat, in order to send fresh troops against a fresh enemy, or to use fresh troops to defeat a weakened force. This is not the case in strategy, however. As we have already shown, once strategy has achieved a success, it need not fear so great a reaction, because that success puts an end to the crisis, and not all strategic forces have necessarily been *weakened*. Only those forces that were *tactically* in the conflict with the enemy forces, that is, those involved in the partial engagement, are weakened by it. . . . Corps that, owing to the numerical superiority of forces, fought little or not at all, and participated merely through their very presence, remain just as they were before the decision, and can be used for new purposes just as though they had been entirely idle. But it is clear how such corps that provide numerical superiority can contribute to the overall success. In fact, it is not difficult to imagine how they can significantly reduce losses in our forces that are engaged in the tactical conflict.

In strategy, then, if losses do not increase with the number of troops employed, but are in fact often reduced as a result, and if, as is self-evident, the decision is made all the more certain on our behalf, then it naturally follows that one can never employ too many forces, and consequently, that those available for use must be used *simultaneously*. (H&P 206–207; H 391–392)

ECONOMY OF FORCE

The path of reason can seldom be narrowed to a simple line through principles and opinions. There always remains a certain leeway, as is true in all of life's practical arts. There are no abscissas and ordinates for the lines of beauty, and circles and ellipses are not brought into being through their algebraic formulas. The individual taking action, therefore, must at times rely on the sensitive instinctive judgment that, based on his innate acumen and trained by reflection, finds the right course almost unconsciously. At other times, he must simplify the law to its prominent features, which form his rules. At still other times, established methods must become the pole he clings to.

One of these simplified features or mental aids is the viewpoint of always ensuring that all of his forces are working together, or in other words, always bearing in mind that no part of his forces must be idle. Whoever has forces in a place where the enemy does not keep them sufficiently occupied, whoever has part of his troops marching (i.e., lying idle) while the enemy's troops are striking, is managing his forces poorly. In this sense, this is a waste of forces that is even worse than if they were used improperly. When the time comes for action, the first requirement is for all parts to be involved, because even the most inappropriate act occupies and fells a portion of the enemy's forces. (H&P 213; H 401)

Therefore, the smaller the number of forces who have actually engaged in combat, and the larger the number of those who have contributed to the outcome through their mere presence, as reserves, the less likely it is that new forces of our opponent will snatch victory from our hands. The commander and the army that have best succeeded in conducting the engagement with an economy of forces and making the utmost of the mental impact of strong reserves, are on the surest path to victory. In recent times, we must concede great mastery of this approach to the French, especially under the leadership of Bonaparte. (H&P 241; H 443)

ECONOMY OF DESIGN

As to whether a simple attack or a more complex, elaborate one will have the greater impact, the answer is surely the latter if the opponent is assumed to be passive. Each complex attack requires more time, however, and there must be sufficient time for it without a counterattack on one part interfering with the preparations for implementing the whole operation. If the enemy opts for a simpler attack that is carried out in a shorter time, he gains the advantage and renders the grand scheme ineffective. Therefore, in evaluating a complex attack, one must consider all the dangers to which one is

Ockham's Razor

Simplex veri sigillum is the Roman's way of saying KISS (keep it simple, stupid). The Latin proverb's literal meaning—simplicity is the seal of truth—expresses a nearly universal article of faith: that the acid test for truth, be it in science or human affairs, is best rendered by the test of the greatest possible simplicity.

When applied to science and philosophy, the principle has been part of the Western intellectual tradition since Aristotle. It is most commonly referred to as Ockham's Razor, in honor of the brilliant Franciscan scholar William of Ockham (1285–1347). Ockham was a passionate investigator and advocate of logic in the pursuit of truth who applied his convictions to theology with such uncompromising fervor that he was excommunicated from the Catholic Church and later admired by Martin Luther. His expression first stated the principle in the sharply articulated form that has survived to our days: *pluralitas non est ponenda sine necessitate,* "plurality should not be posited without necessity." KISS—in so many words.

Also known as the law of economy or law of parsimony, the principle requires that when choosing between two competing theories that are equally successful in explaining the issue at hand, the simpler one should be given preference. There are at least two different interpretations of how such preference is to be justified. The stronger interpretation asserts that nature itself abhors too much complexity and the simpler theory is hence more likely to be true. (This position is exemplified by Aristotle's original statement: "Nature operates in the shortest way possible.") The weaker interpretation, most clearly articulated by the eminent philosopher Karl Popper and held by most scientists of our days, grants preference to the simpler theory as it is easier to refute if it is unsound. The weaker version is not so much a belief about nature but a methodical choice to benefit the progress of science. Einstein may have given the broadest modern interpretation that will serve scientists as reliably as practitioners. It even has the familiar twist of Clausewitzian dialectics: "Everything should be made as simple as possible, but not simpler."

Clausewitz urges the strategist to consider this principle in yet a somewhat different light, not as a test of veracity, nor as a measure of scientific expediency, but as a matter of practical viability. The question is, of two plans with comparable demands on one's own resources and similar impact on the adversary, which one should we prefer? His answer is intimately connected with his notion of friction. The more complex plan has more embellishments, loose ends, and contingencies; it places greater demands on coordination and is more likely to unravel sooner under the force of friction. Undermining what little control and mastery one has in uncertain strategic situations, complexity may look smart on paper but it amounts to the forfeiture of one's own initiative in the field.

But if simplicity holds the promise of truth in science and success in strategy, why are both commodities so scarce and precious? It soon becomes clear that true simplicity consists of much more than merely ignoring the bewildering complexities of reality, repeating formulas that have worked in the past, or acting without due reflection. These behaviors are but facile simplemindedness. The winning simplicity that we seek, the simplicity of genius, is far more elusive indeed. It is the result of intense mental engagement. The great legal scholar and legendary Supreme Court Justice Oliver Wendell Holmes, Jr. (1841–1935) may have articulated most eloquently, even dialectically, the divide separating the two kinds of simplicity: "I would not give a fig for the simplicity this side of complexity, but I would give my life for the simplicity on the other side of complexity."

exposed during the preparatory stages. The complex attack can be used only if one can be sure that the enemy will not destroy it through a quicker action. Whenever this may be the case, we must opt for the shorter route and condense it down as the nature and situation of the enemy and other circumstances may require. If we leave behind the weak impressions of abstract concepts and turn instead to real-life situations, a quick, brave, and determined enemy will not allow us time for long-range complex actions, even though that is precisely the sort of enemy against whom we most need such abilities. This, it seems to us, establishes the superiority of simple, immediate successes over complex schemes.

But we are not claiming that a simple attack is best—only that we should not lift the arm higher than the time to strike allows, and that the more warlike the opponent, the more this approach will call for direct engagement. Instead of trying to outdo our opponent with intricate plans, we would be better off taking the opposite direction so we remain always a step ahead of him.

When we seek out the ultimate constituents of these contrary propositions, we find that one is cleverness and the other is courage. Now, it is very tempting to think that a moderate amount of courage paired with a large portion of cleverness has a greater effect than a moderate amount of cleverness and a large portion of courage. But to avoid misrepresenting the relationship between these elements and arranging them contrary to logic, we should not place cleverness over courage in matters where danger looms all around and that should be regarded as the real domain of courage. (H&P 228–229; H 425–426)

CENTER OF GRAVITY

Two basic principles cover the whole plan of war and serve as a guide for everything else.

The first is to reduce the essence of the enemy's power to the fewest possible centers of gravity, to one, if possible. The attack against those centers of gravity should be reduced to the fewest possible major operations, again to one, if possible. Finally, all secondary operations should be kept as subordinate as possible. In short, the first principle is to act in as concentrated a manner as possible.

The second principle is to act as quickly as possible, that is, no stopping or detours without sufficient cause. (H&P 617; H 1009)

Four Great Generals

Clausewitz refers to rulers whose importance lay largely in their military accomplishments. The Alexander he refers to here is Alexander III (The Great) of Macedon (died 323 B.C.), who used his strategic skill to create an empire stretching from Greece to India. Gustavus II Adolphus (Vasa) was King of Sweden (born 1594) and a leader in the Protestant cause during the Thirty Years' War (1618 to 1648). He was a brilliant military innovator and field commander who made Sweden a major power. Charles XII was a later Swedish king, considered a great soldier but one who over-reached strategically. His army was destroyed in a protracted invasion of Russia in 1709, and Sweden thereafter declined in importance. For Frederick the Great, see sidebar on page 108.

Success cannot be determined from general causes. It is often the individual causes, which no one who was not present can assess. There are also many moral causes that are never expressed, and even the smallest moves and chance events that appear in history merely as anecdotes are often decisive.

What theory can say about this is that the main point is to keep the predominant conditions of both parties in mind. They will give rise to a certain center of gravity, a center of power and movement upon which everything depends, and the focused blow of all our forces must be directed against this center of gravity.

Small matters always depend on great ones, unimportant matters on important ones, and accidental matters on essentials. We must take this as our guide.

Alexander, Gustavus Adolphus, Charles XII, and Frederick the Great all had their center of gravity in their army. If it had been shattered, they would have been poor performers indeed. In states torn apart by internal factions, the center of gravity is found mainly in the capital. In small states that rely on more powerful ones, the center lies in the ally's army; in alliances, the center lies in the community of interest. In popular uprisings, it lies in the person of the chief leader and in public opinion. The attack must be directed against these things. If the opponent loses his balance, he must not be allowed any time to regain it. The attack must continue to be pressed in that direction. In other words, the victor must attack with all his strength. One will truly strike the enemy to the ground by continually seeking the core of the enemy's strength, not by conquering one of the enemy's provinces in a leisurely manner through superior strength, preferring the sure possession of this small conquest to the risks of a major action.

However, regardless of the key element of the enemy's strength against which we are to focus our operations, defeating and destroying his fighting forces is still the best start, and in any event, a vital step. (H&P 595–596; H 976–977)

There is only one exception to the principle of directing all one's forces against the center of gravity of the enemy force, and that is if secondary operations promise *extraordinary benefits;* but we are assuming that in this case decisive superiority puts us in a position to pursue these operations without risking too much in terms of the main theater.

Therefore, the first consideration in drafting a plan of war is to recognize the centers of gravity of the enemy power, and to reduce them to one, if possible. The second is to combine the forces to be used against that center of gravity in a single major action. (H&P 618–619; H 1011)

The main battle, therefore, is to be viewed as concentrated war, as the center of gravity of the whole war or campaign. Just as the sun's rays combine at the focal point of a concave mirror into a perfect image and the most intense heat, the forces and circumstances of war combine in the main battle for a concentrated, maximum impact. (H&P 258; H 468)

Dynamics of Strategy

SURPRISE

The general effort to achieve relative superiority gives rise to another effort, which must, consequently, be equally general: *surprising the enemy*. This is the basis, more or less, of all operations, because without it superiority at the decisive point is quite inconceivable.

Surprise, then, is the means for achieving superiority, but it must also be viewed as an independent principle, specifically through its psychological impact. When surprise is achieved to a greater extent, the consequences are confusion and a shattering of courage within the enemy. There are numerous examples, great and small, of how these amplify the results. The issue here is not the surprise raid itself, which belongs with the attack, but the effort to surprise the enemy with our general approach, and more particularly with the distribution of our forces.

But regardless of how general, and even indispensable, this effort is, and although it is true that the effort will never be entirely with-

Remaking the Rules

Ambrose Bierce's curious career started as a soldier in the American Civil War and ended with fame as writer and journalist in San Francisco where he was celebrated and feared for his acerbic wit. In 1914, he mysteriously disappeared. His disappearance and the unverified accounts of his crossing into Mexico in search of the Mexican Revolution and Pancho Villa are the starting point of the dreamlike tale woven by Carlos Fuentes, one of Mexico's most accomplished novelists, in *The Old Gringo*. General Arroyo is a young rebel commander in Pancho Villa's Northern Division. Following is a conversation between the novel's protagonist and General Arroyo from *The Old Gringo*.

General Arroyo told him that the Federal army, whose officers had studied in the French Military Academy, were waiting to engage them in formal combat, where they knew all the rules and the guerillas didn't.

"They are like virgins," said the young Mexican general, hard and dark as a glazed pot. "They want to follow the rules. I want to make them."

Arroyo looked directly at the old man and told him that now he had to make a choice. They were going to play a trick on the Federal troops. Half of the rebels were to march across the plain to meet the regular army the way they liked, head on, as they had been taught in their academies. The other half would fan out through the mountains like lizards, you can bet your old ass, Arroyo guffawed sourly, and while the Federales were fighting their formal battle with the decoy guerilla troops on the plain, they would cut their supply lines, attack them from the rear, and catch them like rats in a trap.

"You say I have to make a choice?"

"Yes, Indiana General. Where do you want to be?"

"On the plain," the old man replied without an instant's hesitation. "Not for the glory, you understand, but for the danger."

out impact, it is also true that it rarely succeeds to an *extraordinary* degree, and that the reason for this lies in the nature of the matter. Therefore, we would be pursuing a misconception if we were to believe that a great deal can be accomplished in war through surprise. The idea itself seems very promising, but in its implementation it tends to get caught in the friction of the overall machinery. (H&P 198; H 379–380)

Practically the only advantage of the attack lies in the surprise with which the engagement can be started. Suddenness and inexorability are its strongest features, and when the overthrow of the enemy is at issue, they are quite essential.

Thus theory insists on the shortest route to the goal, and rules out of consideration endless debates about whether to move right or left, here or there. Bonaparte never acted otherwise. His favorite route was always the shortest main road from army to army, or from one capital to the next. (H&P 624; H 1020)

When we expect great effects from the principle of surprise in the course of a campaign, we think of a large-scale activity, quick decisions, and forced marches, which offer the means for achieving those effects. However, the examples of two generals who may be considered the best in this regard, Frederick the Great and Bonaparte, show that even when these elements are present to a great degree, the intended effect is not always achieved. In July 1760, when Frederick the Great so suddenly attacked Lacy from Bautzen and turned toward Dresden, he actually accomplished very little with this whole episode; in fact, his situation was greatly deteriorated by it since Glatz had fallen in the interim.

In 1813, Bonaparte twice turned suddenly from Dresden against Blücher, not to mention his invasion of Bohemia from Upper Lusatia. On both occasions, the effects were not what he expected. They were blows in thin air that merely cost him time and strength, and—at Dresden—might have been extremely dangerous. (H&P 199; H 381–382)

A highly successful surprise, in this area as well, is not the result of mere activity, strength, and determination on the part of the leadership; there must also be other contributing circumstances. However, we do not wish to deny that it can be successful. We merely wish to make the connection to the need for favorable circumstances, which of course are not a common occurrence, and which the person acting in war can seldom bring about.

These same generals provide a striking example. First there was Bonaparte's famous operation against Blücher's army in 1814, when it was separated from the main army and marching down the Marne. It would be difficult for a surprise two-day march to accomplish more.

Blücher's army, spread out over the distance of a three-day march, was defeated in separate actions, sustaining a loss equaling that of a major engagement. This was entirely the effect of surprise, since Blücher would have organized his march in an entirely different way if he had been aware of an imminent attack by Bonaparte. Success was linked to this mistake on Blücher's part. Yet Bonaparte was unaware of these circumstances, and so this was truly a stroke of luck for him.

The same is true of the battle of Liegnitz in 1760.

Frederick the Great won that fine battle because he changed his position again during the night, from one that he had only just occupied. Thus Laudon was completely surprised, and lost 70 canon and 10,000 men as a result. Although Frederick at the time had adopted the principle of moving about frequently, in order to render battle impossible or at least to sow confusion in the enemy's plans, the change in position in the night of the 14th to 15th was

Napoleon, Frederick, and Fortune

Clausewitz's comment on Napoleon and Blücher is uncharacteristic, since he is generally skeptical of Napoleon's operations in 1814 and since that campaign resulted in Napoleon's defeat and abdication. However, Napoleon's tactical conduct of the campaign is widely considered brilliant. Maneuvering about between several superior armies invading France, he repeatedly defeated each, often through tactical surprise. He was finally defeated by his strategic mistakes, that is, having provoked a large and powerful coalition against himself and having refused to accept a favorable diplomatic settlement when it was offered to him.

At Liegnitz, Frederick cut his way out of a joint Austrian-Russian encirclement by a night attack in an unexpected locale, then tricked the Russians into retreating with a false message indicating that the Austrian army had been totally destroyed. Clausewitz's point is that Frederick changed positions for reasons entirely unconnected with his decision to attack the Austrians, but the change in position decisively contributed to the success of his attack. This was chance, not brilliance, at work.

not made specifically for that purpose. Rather, as the king himself said, the reason was merely that the position taken up on the 14th displeased him. Here again, chance was once again very much involved. The outcome would not have been the same without the coincidence of the attack with the nighttime change of position, and the inaccessibility of the location.

Now there is still one comment to be made concerning the heart of the matter, and that is that only the party that sets the rules for the other can create surprise, and the party acting correctly sets the rules. If we surprise our enemy with an incorrect move, we may suffer a severe setback rather than enjoy a favorable outcome. In any event, the enemy need not be terribly concerned with our surprise; he will find in our mistake the means to ward off this evil.

Moltke on Chance and Luck

To the calculation of a known and an unknown quantity—namely one's own will and that of the enemy—enter yet other factors. These are the fully unforeseeable: weather, illnesses, railway accidents, misunderstandings and disappointments—in short, all the influences that one may call luck, fate, or higher providence, which mankind neither creates nor dominates.

Nevertheless, the conduct of war does not lapse into blind, arbitrary action. A calculation of probabilities shows that all those chance happenings are just as often to the detriment or advantage of the one side as they are to the other. . . .

It is obvious that theoretical knowledge does not suffice for this. On the contrary, both mental faculties and character are necessary for this free, practical, artistic activity, schooled obviously by military training and guided by experience, either from military history or from life itself.

Success, above all, determines the reputation of a supreme commander. How much of this is really earned is extraordinarily difficult to determine. . . . Nevertheless, in the long run only the intelligent have good luck. (Hughes, 1993)

The sheer number of important discoveries made by the French chemist and microbiologist Louis Pasteur may have made him more generous than the average mortal in acknowledging the role of chance and good luck in his achievements. This he freely did, freely did, at the risk of having his accomplishments belittled, but not without famously reminding those who would do so that "Luck favors the prepared mind."

This fortuitous but strange companionship of luck and intellect did not escape Moltke's attention either; he too was a man of great stature who had been granted both a sharp mind and good fortune.

> Whether in war, science, or business, the intellect that demands certainty as a condition for taking the next step will be a timid or petulant but ultimately sterile intellect. Chance and the unexpected provide the richest setting to engage the intellect.

Much depends on the general circumstances in which both parties stand with respect to each other. If one is already in a position to intimidate and outpace the other through his general moral superiority, he will be better able to exploit the element of surprise and will achieve good results even where he should actually have met with disaster. (H&P 200–201; H 382–384)

ALLIANCES

The ancient republics, with the exception of Rome, were small. Their armies were even smaller, since the great masses, the common people, were excluded. These republics were so numerous and so close together that the natural balance into which small unattached parts always fall, in keeping with a general law of nature, was bound to pose an obstacle for them with regard to great undertakings. So their wars were limited to laying waste open countryside and capturing individual cities, in order to attain a certain measure of influence there in the future.

The single exception to this rule was Rome, but only in its later period. Rome long used small groups to fight its neighbors in the usual battle for spoils and alliances. It grew large not so much through conquest as through the alliances it formed, in which neighboring peoples gradually united with Rome to form a larger whole. It was only after Rome had spread throughout southern Italy in this way that it truly began to advance by conquest. (H&P 586–587; H 962–963)

In European politics, states traditionally enter into offensive and defensive mutual assistance alliances, but not so much so that the disputes and interests of one party thereby become those of the other. Rather they promise in advance to provide each other with a certain, and generally quite modest, level of military force, without regard to the object of the war and the efforts of the enemy. In such alliances, an ally does not consider itself engaged in an actual war with the enemy, which would entail a declaration of war at the outset and a peace treaty at the conclusion. But even this concept, too, has never been worked out with great clarity and its usage varies.

This matter would have a sort of internal coherence, and the theory of war would be put in a less embarrassing situation, if the promised 10,000, 20,000, or 30,000 men were given over entirely to the state at war so that it could use those forces as it saw fit. Then these forces could be considered hired troops. What happens in practice, however, is a quite different matter. The auxiliary troops generally have their own commander, who reports only to his own government, which sets the commander's objectives as best suits its own halfhearted aims. (H&P 603; H 987–988)

But even when two states actually go to war against a third, they are not always so explicit as to say, "We must view this third party as our enemy, whom we must destroy or risk being destroyed in return." Rather, the matter is often handled like a commercial transaction. Each party invests 30,000 to 40,000 men in accordance with the risks to which it is exposed and the advantages it expects to achieve, and then acts as though that were all it stood to lose.

This approach is not limited to occasions when one state comes to the assistance of another in a matter that is rather irrelevant to it. It also occurs when both share a considerable interest. Diplomatic caution guides every move, and negotiators are careful to commit only a small auxiliary force under the treaty terms so that they may use their remaining military force to suit particular needs that may arise from policy considerations. (H&P 603; H 988)

How very different is the cohesion between that of an army rallying around *one* flag carried into battle at the personal command of *one* general and that of an *allied military force* extending 50 or 100 leagues, or even on different sides of the theater! In the first case, cohesion is at its strongest and unity at its closest. In the second case, the unity is very remote, often consisting of no more than a shared political intention, and therefore only scanty and imperfect, while the cohesion of the parts is mostly weak and often no more than an illusion. (H&P 486; H 810)

EXPLOITING TENSION

Real action is always interrupted by longer or shorter pauses, making it necessary for us to examine the nature of these two conditions.

When military action is suspended, that is, when neither of the two parties wants anything positive, the result is rest and equilibrium; this, of course, is equilibrium in the broadest sense, referring not only to physical and moral forces, but to all circumstances and interests as well. When one of the two parties does set itself a new positive goal, and takes action to achieve it, if only in the form of preparations, and as soon as the adversary opposes this, a tension of forces occurs. It lasts until the decision is made, that is, until one of the two gives up its goal, or the other has conceded it to him. (H&P 221; H 414)

When there is tension, the decision is always more effective, partly because greater force of will and greater pressure of circumstances are revealed, and partly because everything is already prepared and arranged for a major movement. In such cases, the decision is like the effects of a well-concealed and buried mine, whereas an event of perhaps equal significance that takes place during a period of rest is more or less like a mass of powder that explodes in the open air. (H&P 221; H 415)

Now, the essential point we derive from this observation is the conclusion that any measure taken during a state of tension is more important and yields greater results than would have been the case if that same measure had been taken at a time of equilibrium. And as the tension mounts, the importance continues to increase without limit.

We consider it a major requirement for a general to recognize these states properly and to have the acuity to act on that information. The campaign of 1806 shows us just how sorely these desiderata are at times lacking. At a time of enormous tension, when everything was pressing in toward a major resolution, and every fiber of the general's being should have been attuned to that tension and its consequences, measures were proposed, and partly enacted (the reconnaissance mission to Franconia), that in a state of equilibrium would have produced at most a minor back-and-forth exchange. In the thick of these confusing, time-consuming measures and considerations, the necessary measures—the ones that alone could have saved the day—were lost.

Everything pertaining to the relationship between attack and defense and the execution of this two-sided act has to do with the state of crisis—a state in which the forces are engulfed in tension and movement. Furthermore, we consider all activity that can occur in a state of equilibrium a mere corollary and will deal with it as such, since the crisis constitutes the actual war, and the equilibrium is only a reflection of it. (H&P 222; H 415–416)

THE CULMINATION POINT

The victor is not able to defeat his adversary completely in every war. Often, and in most cases, there is a culminating point of victory. The bulk of experience has demonstrated this at length. But since this topic is particularly important for the theory of war and is the supporting point for almost all campaign plans, and because its surface is clouded by an array of apparent contradictions as though by a dis-

Borodino

Leo Tolstoy — *War and Peace;* Book 13, Chapter II

As Napoleon advanced towards Moscow in 1812, the Russians retreated before his armies. The two forces finally clashed at Borodino, and both sides suffered horrendous losses (the Russians lost 45,000 out of 120,000; the French, 30,000 out of 130,000). After the encounter, the Russians, under Kutuzov, retreated and refused to reengage the French. Shortly thereafter, Napoleon occupied Moscow unopposed. But despite the larger Russian losses at Borodino, and the fact that the French were left in possession of the field, the battle is often read as the point at which Napoleon finally sealed his fate in Russia by fatally overextending his attack — by continuing forward after passing its culminating point. Tolstoy, in *War and Peace,* describes the aftermath and consequence of the battle as follows:

> Having rolled like a ball in the direction of the impetus given by the whole campaign and by the battle of Borodino, the Russian army — when the strength of that impetus was exhausted and no fresh push was received — assumed the position natural to it.
>
> Kutuzov's merit lay, not in any strategic maneuver of genius, as it is called, but in the fact that he alone understood the significance of what had happened. He alone then understood the meaning of the French army's inactivity, he alone continued to assert that the battle of Borodino had been a victory, he alone — who as commander in chief might have been expected to be eager to attack — employed his whole strength to restrain the Russian army from useless engagements.
>
> The beast wounded at Borodino was lying where the fleeing hunter had left him; but whether he was still alive, whether he was strong and merely lying low, the hunter did not know. Suddenly the beast was heard to moan.
>
> The moan of that wounded beast (the French army) which betrayed its calamitous condition was the sending of Lauriston to Kutuzov's camp with overtures for peace.

play of shimmering colors, we wish to take a closer look at it, and to address its internal logic. (H&P 566; H 935)

It takes time for every physical force in nature to be effective. A force that would be sufficient to stop a body in motion when applied slowly and gradually will be overcome by it if the time it requires is lacking. This law of nature is an appropriate image for many of the phenomena in our inner lives. If we are stirred to follow a certain train of thought, there are not many things that can change or stop it, no matter how intrinsically capable they may be of doing so. That takes time, rest, and a sustained impact on our consciousness. The same is true in war. Once the mind has settled on a particular direction forward toward the goal or back toward a refuge, it is easy for the reasons that compel one man to stop, and motivate another man to action, not to be felt to their fullest extent. Since the action continues in the meantime, one crosses the limits of equilibrium, moving beyond the culmination point without being aware of it.

It can even happen that the attacker, buoyed by the moral forces that lie particularly in the attack, will find it less tiresome to keep forging ahead, despite the exhaustion of his forces, than to stop— like a horse dragging a load uphill. We believe that this shows logically how the attacker can move beyond the point that, were he to stop and take up the defense, still offers him good results, that is, beyond the point of equilibrium. Therefore, in planning the campaign, it is important to take adequate account of this point, both for the attacker, so that he will not take actions beyond his abilities and run up a debt, as it were, and for the defender, so that he will recognize and take advantage of this mistake when the attacker makes it. (H&P 572; H 944–945)

Overshooting this goal is not simply a *pointless* expenditure of effort leading to no further gains. Rather, it a *destructive* action that causes reactions, and broad experience has shown that these reactions have a disproportional impact. This is such a common occurrence, and seems so natural and readily understandable, that we can dispense with a detailed analysis of its root causes. In every case, the most important of these are a lack of organization in the newly taken country and the psychological impact caused by the profound incongruity between a significant loss and the new gains that were expected.

Moral strength and encouragement often rising to the level of bravado, on the one hand, and despondency, on the other hand, here commonly play against each other in an exceptionally dynamic way. Thus losses during the retreat are increased, and those on the retreat usually thank heaven if they get away with giving back what they had taken without suffering losses of their own territory.

At this point, we must clear up an apparent contradiction that is beginning to take shape. One would think, of course, that so long as there is progress being made as the attack moves forward there must still be superiority of strength, and since the defense that begins at the conclusion of this victorious progression is a stronger form of war than the attack there is all the less danger of suddenly becoming the weaker party. Yet the danger is there. If we look back over history, we must concede that often the greatest danger of reversal does not occur until the moment at which the attack eases up and transitions into defense. (H&P 570–571; H 942)

THE EVOLUTION OF STRATEGY

War Models

The consideration that must be given to the nature of war today has a major impact on all planning, particularly on strategic planning.

Bonaparte's luck and audacity have disrupted all the earlier customary approaches and first-rate nations have been wiped out nearly with one blow. Through their persistent fighting, the Spaniards have shown what can be achieved by arming a nation and insurrection on a vast scale, despite their weakness and slackness with regard to details. In its campaign of 1812, Russia taught us first that an empire of such vast dimensions cannot be conquered (which might readily have been known beforehand), and second that the probability of success does not necessarily decrease in proportion to one's losses of battles, capitals, and provinces (which all previous diplomats accepted as irrefutable truth, and prompted them to conclude a provisional, albeit bad, peace). Rather, it taught us that one is often strongest at the heart of one's own country, when the enemy's offensive strength has been exhausted; and it has shown us with what enormous energy the defensive can switch over to the offensive.

Guerilla Warfare

Napoleon had repeatedly defeated the regular armies of several first-rate military powers—as well as those of Spain (which was not a first-rate power)—in decisive battles and campaigns. In Spain, however, he was later defeated by a slow, persistent, decentralized guerilla war (which he called the Spanish Ulcer) waged by a largely undirected population. This was an utter surprise to all observers. Napoleon actually lost as many troops in Spain between 1808 and 1814 as he lost in Russia in the campaign of 1812 to 1813.

Clausewitz was one of the earliest military thinkers to recognize that guerilla wars waged by local insurgents are a natural outgrowth of warfare as it came to be practiced in the era of the French Revolution and Napoleon. Such wars were an inevitable consequence of war's transformation from limited territorial conflicts between aristocratic states to titanic struggles between nations putting their full resources behind massive conscripted armies. Clausewitz warned that guerilla warfare is a reasonable mode of war only under very specific circumstances (for example, against an occupying army, in rough and inaccessible terrain, and in a protracted resistance rather than a pitched battle). Nevertheless, his analysis of Napoleon's misfortunes in Spain, and to some extent in Russia, gave him a clear understanding of the extent to which guerilla action can ultimately pose a serious threat to the strongest regular army. His image of guerillas as "smoldering embers" that eat away at the edges of an enemy army would come to seem prescient in light of the revolutions, people's wars, and partisan resistance of the twentieth century.

As the reader may have noticed and critics of Clausewitz will never cease to point out, *On War* is virtually silent on what is commonly understood as technology. At least one scholar of Clausewitz has made the far more penetrating observation that Clausewitz had identified the most eminent and enduring technological innovation of his time: guerilla warfare.* It may strike us as a little incongruous at first that small bands of poorly trained and equipped recruits from among the most downtrodden in a country's population should be equated with high tech, but our concern should be strategic leverage and impact—not with appearances.

In the absence of effective protection of intellectual property, for example, technological innovations incorporated in weapons, equipment, and other novel hardware, such innovations were copied quickly in Clausewitz's time and could certainly not be denied effectively to a resourceful opponent in war. Thus the hardware edge was transient at best and of doubtful value in strategy. Innovations in software, such as the ability to channel and mold the wrath, energy, and motivation of civilians into "smoldering embers" of devastating force, was and continues to be a source of advantage that is nearly impossible to imitate or parry adequately.

Hard is soft and soft is hard as Herbert Simon has observed in a different context (the sciences) but in the same spirit.

In business we do not encounter guerillas in the strict sense, but we must be aware of the enormous power that resides in engaging the customer in the value creation process. This has taken many forms and is not altogether different from guerilla warfare. Whether I wear a company's logo on my shirt or whether I submit my commentaries on a company's beta version software, I have made a choice to actively support a cause and to deny my support to others. Such an alliance between regular and irregular troops in business is just as hard to imitate or parry as it is in war.

*W. B. Gallie, *Philosophers of Peace and War: Kant, Clausewitz, Marx, Engels, and Tolstoy* (New York: Cambridge University Press, 1978), p. 65.

The Prussians at Jena

At Jena in 1806, the Prussian army attempted to use the same stratagem Frederick had used in 1757 at Leuthen. Unfortunately, the trick was now well known, and in any case the army of Napoleon was able to deal with it easily. Whereas Frederick's army had been more mobile than its enemies (a key factor in the success of this tactic), in 1806 the French were the masters of battlefield mobility, and the Prussians were utterly crushed.

Remarkably, Clausewitz was among the first to recognize the significance of the Battle of Jena. Only a few months later, he published three letters on its momentous military and political implications.

Moreover, in 1813 Prussia showed us that sudden efforts can multiply the usual strength of an army sixfold, by means of a militia, and that this militia can be used just as well outside the country as inside it.

All these examples show what a significant factor the heart and feelings of a nation are in its overall political, war-related, and general military strength. Since governments have come to understand all these additional resources, we cannot expect that they will be left unused in future wars. (H&P 220; H 412–413)

What is more natural than that the French Revolution had its own way of doing things, and what theory could ever have been capable of including that particular approach? The evil is only that such an approach that derives from this particular case easily outlives its day; it carries on while the circumstances in which it arose change imperceptibly. This is what theory should prevent, through lucid and rational criticism. In 1806, the Prussian generals Prince Louis at Saalfeld, Tauentzien on the Dornberg near Jena, Grawert on one side of Kapellendorf, and Rüchel on the other all threw themselves into the jaws of destruction using the oblique battle order of Frederick the Great. This was not merely an approach that had long outlived its usefulness; no, it was the most absolute poverty of mind that devotion to method ever produced. It managed to destroy Hohenlohe's army in a way that no other army had ever been destroyed on the battlefield. (H&P 154–155; H 311)

Dictates of the Age

Louis XIV, even though it was his intention to upset the entire balance of power in Europe, and at the end of the seventeenth century found himself in a position where he was not terribly concerned about the general enmity he faced, conducted war in the time-honored manner. Although his military force was that of the greatest and richest monarch, in terms of its makeup it was just like the others.

Plundering and laying waste to the enemy's territory, which had played such a major role among the Tartars and the ancient peoples and even during the Middle Ages, were no longer in keeping with the spirit of the age. These actions were rightly considered unnecessarily brutish, something that could easily be avenged and that affected the enemy's subjects more than the enemy government. Therefore, they were ineffective and served only to hold back cultural development. So war was increasingly limited to the army itself, not only in terms of its means, but also in terms of its objectives. The army, with its fortresses and a few prepared positions, formed a state within the state, within which militarism slowly subsided.

All Europe rejoiced at this development, and understood it as a necessary consequence of intellectual advances. This was incorrect, however. Intellectual advance can never lead to a contradiction, can never make two plus two equal five, as we have said before and will repeat again. Nonetheless, this change did have a positive effect on the people. We must not overlook the fact that it made war, to an even greater extent, a merely governmental matter, distancing it even more from the interests of the people. At that time, the war plan of a state, when it was the attacker, consisted mainly of seizing one or another enemy province. The defender's plan was to prevent this. The solitary plan of campaign was to take the enemy's fortress, or to prevent one's own from being taken. A battle was sought and engaged in only when absolutely unavoidable. Anyone who sought a battle without this inevitability, from a sheer internal drive for victory, was considered a bold general indeed. Generally a campaign was over with a single siege, or two if it was a major event. In winter quarters, which were deemed a necessity for both sides, the poor condition of one party could not be considered an advantage for the other; there was almost no contact at all between the sides. These winter quarters definitely limited the action that was to occur during a campaign.

If the forces were too closely balanced, or if the party initiating the action was clearly the weaker of the two, there would be no battle or siege. The whole action of a campaign boiled down to maintaining certain positions and magazines, and regularly securing resources from certain locations.

As long as war was generally fought this way, and the natural limitations of its power were so immediate and visible, no one found anything contradictory in it; rather, they considered everything to be in fine order. Criticism, which began to turn its attention to the art of war in the eighteenth century, was directed toward individual issues, paying scant attention to the start and end of war. Thus there was greatness and perfection of all sorts, and even Field Marshal Daun, a major reason for Frederick the Great's success in achieving his objectives and for Maria Theresa's failure to achieve hers, could be considered a great general. Only occasionally did some penetrating judgment come along, the insights of sound common sense, noting that something positive was to be gained through superiority of numbers, or that the war was being poorly managed despite the art displayed.

This is how matters stood when the French Revolution broke out. Austria and Prussia tried their diplomatic art of war, which quickly proved inadequate. Viewing the situation from the conventional perspective, hopes focused on a greatly weakened military force, but in 1793 there appeared a force beyond any previous imagination. Suddenly war was once again a matter for the people, indeed a people 30 million strong, all of whom considered themselves citizens of the state. Without examining in detail the particular circumstances that accompanied this great event, we shall merely examine the relevant results. As the people now participated in the war, it was no longer a cabinet and an army, but the natural weight of the whole population that was brought to bear. From then on, the means used and the efforts made no longer had any specific limit; the energy with which the war itself could be conducted no longer had a counterweight, and consequently the danger for the enemy was extreme indeed.

The reason the whole revolutionary war played out before all this was fully felt and became quite evident, and the reason the revolutionary generals did not advance inexorably toward their final goal and shatter the European monarchies, and why the German armies from time to time had occasion to resist successfully and put a halt to the French path to victory, really lay in the technical imperfections the French had to fight against. These imperfections were first clear among the common soldiers, then among the generals, and, at the time of the Directory, within the government itself.

Once all this had been perfected in Bonaparte's hands, this vast military power—borne upon the strength of the entire nation—swept across Europe in a wave of destruction with such assuredness and reliability that wherever it encountered only the old form of military power there was never a moment's doubt about the outcome. A reaction came in due course. Of its own accord, the war became a concern of the people in Spain. In Austria in 1809, the government first engaged in extraordinary efforts with reserves and militia; these drew close to their objective and outstripped anything Austria had previously thought feasible. In 1812, Russia took the examples of Spain and Austria as its model. The vast size of that empire enabled its preparations, though late, to be effective nonetheless, and increased their impact as well. The result was brilliant. In

Germany, Prussia was the first to pull itself together, making the war a concern of the people; with half as many inhabitants as before the war and no money or credit at all, it fielded forces that were twice as numerous as those in 1806. The rest of Germany sooner or later took the field with unaccustomed force, following the examples of Prussia and Austria, though making less of an effort than in 1809. So it was that in 1813 and 1814, Germany and Russia fielded approximately a million men against the French counting all those who took part and those who were killed in the two campaigns.

Under these circumstances, the energy involved in conducting the war was quite different as well. Even though this energy only at times equaled that of the French, and on other occasions timidity prevailed, nonetheless the campaigns were generally conducted in the new style, not the old. In eight months, the theater of war shifted from the Oder to the Seine; proud Paris bowed its head for the first time, and the formidable Bonaparte lay in chains.

After Bonaparte, then, war took on an entirely different character as it once again became a concern of the people—first on one side and then on the other. War drew very close to its true nature, its absolute perfection. There were no longer any visible limits to the means at hand; any limits disappeared in the energy and enthusiasm of the governments and their subjects. The energy that went into the conduct of war was increased immensely by the vast range of means and the broad field of possible results, and by the powerful stirring of feelings. The aim of military action was to defeat the enemy; it was not until the enemy lay helpless on the ground that it was deemed possible to stop and reach agreement on the opponents' objectives.

So it was that the warlike element, freed from all conventional restraints, broke loose with all its natural force. The reason was the involvement of the people in this great affair of state. This involvement sprang in part from the wide-ranging effects of the French Revolution, and in part from the danger that all nations faced from the French.

Adaptability and Prussian Policy

Prussia had lost half of its territory and population in the peace settlement that followed her defeats in 1806 and 1807. Also, Napoleon had sharply limited the size permitted the Prussian army. Prussian military reformers like Scharnhorst and Gneisenau (and Clausewitz) got around these problems by training large numbers of short-term militia, thus creating a large, quasi-official reserve force of partially trained local troops with middle-class officers that could be called up on relatively short notice. This utterly contradicted the Prussian tradition of using highly trained professional forces consisting mostly of foreign recruits and the dregs of Prussia's own society, officered entirely by long-service officers from the noble classes. But it worked. Prussia was able to greatly increase the size of its army in a very short time after declaring war on Napoleon in 1813. And although militia had traditionally been used only for local defense, the Prussians were able to incorporate the new forces into the regular army and use them in the ensuing invasion of France. The model for this development was probably the mass conscription of the French army, not the guerilla resistance in Spain. And the social implications horrified Prussia's traditional leaders, who feared it would lead to bloody revolution by the now-armed lower and middle classes. But it worked.

It is difficult to tell whether all future wars in Europe will be conducted with the full weight of the state, and consequently will occur only when matters of great interest to the people are at stake; or whether gradually once again the interests of the government and the people will drift apart. We do not presume to settle the matter here. No one would disagree, however, if we were to say that once limits—which exist, so to speak, only in an unawareness of what is possible—are struck down, they are not easily rebuilt. At least when vital issues are at stake, mutual hostility will be resolved as it has been in our age.

This brings our historical overview to a close. Our purpose was not hastily to assign a few principles for the conduct of war to every age, but merely to indicate how each age has its own form of war, its own limiting conditions, and its own biases. The events of every age, therefore, must be judged in light of the peculiarities of the period. Only a person who can position himself within the context of the period, not through meticulous study of details so much as through an accurate look at the broader picture, is able to understand and assess its generals.

Yet this conduct of war, although conditioned by the particular situations of states and their military forces, must still contain something more general, or rather something quite general, that theory should address above all else.

This recent period when war reached its absolute strength most clearly exhibits what is generally valid and necessary. Yet it is as improbable that henceforth all wars will have this massive quality as it is that the wide latitude opened up for war could once again be closed off entirely. In a theory that focused solely on this absolute form of war, one would either have to ignore or condemn as errors any instances in which outside influences changed the nature of war. This cannot be the object of theory; rather, theory should focus on what the real—not the ideal—circumstances of war are. By training its investigating, discriminating, and categorizing gaze on such matters, theory always has within its view the wide variety of circumstances that can give rise to war. It will lay down the broad outlines of war so that there is sufficient room for the needs of the age and for the needs of the moment.

Accordingly we must say that the goal a party that undertakes war sets for itself, and the means it uses to achieve it, are guided by the particular characteristics of its situation; but they will also be affected by the character of the age and its general circumstances; finally, *it will continue to be subject to the general conclusions that must be drawn from the nature of war.* (H&P 590–594; H 969–974)

THE VIRTUES OF STRATEGY

*In which all the clever thinking that can be done in strategy
must humbly and courteously
leave the stage
in deference
to moral strengths and qualities.
At the heart of strategy,
there must be a heart
that knows what to do with strategy.*

Moral Forces

Moral forces are among the most important topics of war. They are the spirit that permeates the entire aspect of war; they adhere more quickly and more readily to the will, which sets into motion and guides the entire panoply of forces. At the same time, they merge as one with the will, because the will is itself a moral force. Unfortunately, they are not the sort of thing that can be codified in books, because they resist being grouped by number or class. They prefer to be seen or felt.

The spirit and other moral qualities of an army, of a general, and of governments, the disposition of the provinces in which a war is waged, the moral effect of victory or defeat, are all intrinsically different, and their relation to our goal and our circumstances can also have a great variety of effects.

Even though books have little or nothing to say about the topic, these issues belong as much to theory on the art of war as anything else associated with war. For as I have said before and will say again, it is a poor philosophy that excludes moral forces from its rules and principles, as was done in the old school, and that begins to count those forces as exceptions whenever they make an appearance. It is equally bad if we seek a solution by appealing to genius, which transcends all rules, thus implying not only that rules are written for foolish people, but that they themselves must be foolish.

Even if theory on the art of war did nothing more than to call this topic to mind, if it demonstrated the necessity of acknowledging the full worth of moral forces and the need to take those forces into consideration, it would already be taking the realm of spirit under its mantle. Armed with this viewpoint, it would summarily condemn anyone arguing his case before it who invoked only the physical relationship of forces.

Furthermore, with respect to all other so-called rules, theory cannot close its borders to the moral forces, because the effects of physical forces are entirely fused with the effects of the moral forces. They cannot be separated, like some metal alloy submitted to a chemical process. Each rule that makes reference to physical forces must call to mind the role in theory that the moral forces may play if theory is to avoid taking a detour into categorical propositions, which are at times too timid and limited and at other times overbearing and overambitious. Even the most matter-of-fact theories have inadvertently let themselves stray into this area. For example, one cannot explain the effects of a victory without in some way taking into consideration the moral impressions. In fact, most of the subjects covered in this book are a combination of causes and effects that are half physical and half moral. One might say that the physical is almost like the wood handle, the moral like the fine metal, which together constitute a well-made, brightly polished weapon.

The value of moral forces in general and the sometimes incredible influence they exert are best seen through examples from history; this is the most noble and most excellent means of self-instruction the general can employ. This shows us that demonstrations, critical investigations, and learned treatises are less valuable than feelings, general impressions, and specific flashes of insight when it comes to cultivating the soul with the seeds of wisdom.

We could go one by one through the most important moral phenomena in war and with the meticulousness of a professor see what can be said about each of them, either good or bad. But it is too easy to come up with banal observations employing that method, while the mind proper degenerates into analysis, so that we unwittingly wind up saying things that everyone knows. Consequently, we preferred to take a more incomplete, rhapsodical approach than usual, in general touching on the importance of the issue and indicating the spirit that informs our viewpoints in this book. (H&P 184–185; H 356–358)

The principal moral powers are as follows: the *talents of the general*, *military excellence of the army*, and *popular sentiment of the army*. Which of these has more value is hard to say in general, because we encounter enough difficulty trying to say anything about their magnitude, let alone to weigh the magnitude of one against the magnitude of another. Ideally, we should not shortchange any one of them, as human judgment is inclined to do, whimsically darting from one to another. Instead, we should acknowledge the unmistakable power of these three elements by examining the ample evidence of history.

Nevertheless, it is true that of late all the armies of European states appear to be at the same point of development in their internal discipline and preparation. Warfare has become, to use an expression of the philosophers, so "in accordance with nature" that it is now something of a method that all armies seem to possess, so that even a general's deployment of special means, in the narrow sense (like Frederick II's oblique battle lines), no longer has much to offer. Thus, as things now stand, popular sentiment and an army's habituation to war undeniably play a much larger role. A long period of peace could change that.

The popular sentiment of an army (enthusiasm, fanatic zeal, faith, public opinion) shows itself to advantage in mountain campaigns, where each man is on his own, down to the last soldier. Consequently, the mountains make the best battleground for a campaign mobilizing the citizenry.

Skillful execution and a courage of steel, which bind the troops together as though they were cast from one mold, are most effective out in the open.

Average, hilly terrain is most suited for demonstrating the general's talent. In the mountains, the general does not have enough control over the individual parts and cannot lead everyone. A campaign in the open is too easy and does not sufficiently tap his capabilities.

Plans should be chosen with these unmistakable correlations in mind. (H&P 186; H 359–360)

The Virtues of the Army

MORAL AND PHYSICAL

Military virtues are to be distinguished from mere bravery, and even more so from an enthusiasm for matters of war. Bravery is obviously a necessary component of military excellence. But though ordinary people may have a natural disposition for bravery, a soldier can cultivate bravery as a member of an army through habituation and drills, and it must also take a different direction than is found in the ordinary person. It must be stripped of the impulse characteristic of an individual to do whatever he wants and to use displays of force. Instead, it must submit to higher-level commands, obedience, order, rule, and method. An enthusiasm for matters of war is not a necessary component, even though it does give life and increased vigor to the military excellence of an army.

War—regardless of how broad its reach or whether it calls into service every man fit to bear arms—is a specific type of matter, separate and distinct from the other activities humans carry out. To be imbued with the spirit and essence of this matter; to awaken, culti-

vate, and endow oneself with the powers that it requires; to delve
into it fully with the intellect; to achieve sureness and dexterity in
its ways through practice; to become wholly subsumed by it; to shed
the role of an ordinary human and assume the role assigned
therein—that specifically is the military excellence of an army.

No matter how carefully we might attempt to nurture the citi-
zen alongside the soldier in the selfsame individual, no matter how
much we may try to nationalize wars, and no matter how much we
may think things have changed since the days of the condottieri, the
role of the individual in the process of war can never be eliminated.
And if that is so, those who carry out that process, for as long as
they carry it out, will always regard themselves as a type of corporate body whose regulations, laws, and practices primarily create the
spirit of the war. And so in fact they do. But even if we were determined to consider war from the highest standpoint, we would be
very wrong to underestimate the *esprit de corps* that an army can and
must have to some degree. Beneath the natural forces at work
within, this *esprit de corps* provides a certain element of cohesion to
the military excellence of an army. The *esprit de corps* allows military
excellence to crystallize more readily.

An army that keeps its usual order under the most punishing
fire; that never takes fright from an imaginary fear; that in the face
of real danger battles for every inch of ground; that never abandons
its obedience, even in the midst of ruinous defeat, out of assurance
that it will prevail; that does not lose its confidence in its leaders or
its respect for them; whose physical powers, like the muscles of an
athlete, are strengthened through deprivation and exertion; that
regards these strenuous demands as a means toward victory and not
as a rout; that takes refuge in its flag; and that in all of these duties
and virtues heeds the short catechism of a single notion, namely, to
honor one's arms: This is an army imbued with military excellence.

Armies can strike mighty blows like the Vendéans or accomplish
great feats like the Swiss, Americans, or Spanish without displaying
this military excellence; leaders can successfully command standing

armies, like Eugene and Marlborough, without its help. Therefore, let it not be said that a successful war is inconceivable without it. And we should be especially careful to make the concept we have just presented here more concrete, so that these ideas are not lost in a sea of vague generalization, leading someone to think that military excellence is everything. That is not true. The military excellence of an army is manifested as a definite moral power, which can be extracted by thought and its effect evaluated—like a tool whose power can be calculated.

Now that we have characterized military excellence in this way, let us see what can be said about its influence and about the means of acquiring it.

Military virtue is to each of the individual parts what the genius of the general is to the whole. The general can lead only the whole, not each of its individual parts—and when he cannot lead an individual part, the military spirit has to step in as leader. The general is chosen by his reputation for outstanding qualities, and higher-ranking leaders of large troops are chosen by an even more stringent test. But this testing diminishes the further down in the ranks we look, until at the level of the masses, specific qualities do not enter the picture. And yet it is precisely those nonspecific qualities that must take the place of military excellence. Filling that role are the natural qualities of a people mobilized for war: *valor, skillfulness,* a *willingness to endure hardship,* and *zeal.* Those traits can replace the military spirit and vice versa. (H&P 187–188; H 361–363)

This spirit comes from only two sources, both of which are necessary for its existence. The first is a string of wars and victories, and the other an active army frequently driven to the height of exertion. Only under these circumstances does the soldier come to know his true strength. The more a commander demands of his soldiers, the more confident he can be that what he asks will be carried out. A soldier is as proud of the hard work he has endured as of the dangers he has faced. So this seed will flourish only in the soil of constant activity and effort—but also only in the sunlight of victory. Once it has grown into a sturdy tree, it will withstand the strongest storms of misfortune and defeat, and even the sluggish calm of peace, at least for a time. However, it can only *come into being* in war, and under great commanders. It can endure, however, for several generations at least, even under mediocre commanders and during extended periods of peace. (H&P 189; H 364)

We have identified danger, physical exertion, rumor, and friction as elements that come together in the thick of war and hamper all activity. The impediments they raise can be grouped even further under the sweeping concept *general friction*. But is there no oil that can relieve this friction? Only one, and a general and his army cannot summon it at will—it is an army's habituation to war.

Habituation strengthens the body through strenuous exertion, the soul through exposure to great danger, and the judgment through protection against first impressions. Overall, it teaches a valuable prudence, from the hussar and rifleman all the way up to the division general, and simplifies the general's work.

Just as the pupil of the human eye dilates in a dark room, absorbing the little light that is present, and bit by bit distinguishes things dimly until at last it makes out objects clearly, the same can be said of a soldier practiced in war—the novice sees only the pitch black of night. (H&P 122; H 265)

THE LADDER OF ABILITY

There is a great gulf between a general, that is, either an individual in charge of the war overall or a general with responsibility for a theater of war, and the next level of command. The simple reason is that the second in command is subject to much more detailed guidance and oversight, and consequently has many more restrictions on his independent thought. As a result, common opinion holds that exceptional intellectual activity is involved only in the upper echelons, and that average intelligence is sufficient for everything below that. Indeed, it is not uncommon that a subordinate general who has grown gray in the service, whose one-sided activities have led to an unmistakable poverty of mind, will be viewed as somewhat stultified. While they praise his courage, people also smile at his simplemindedness. It is not our intention to fight for a better lot for these men. That would contribute nothing to their effectiveness, and little to their happiness. We wish merely to point out how things really are, and to warn against the error of believing that a brave yet unintelligent man can do something truly first-rate in war.

Now if we consider that exceptional intellectual ability is necessary even at the lowest levels for a person to be deemed exceptional, and that these abilities increase at every stage, it follows, naturally, that we should have an entirely different view of those who hold the rank of second in command in an army and do so with distinction; their apparent simplicity in comparison with a person of great learning, a skillful businessman, or a statesman in conference should not blind us to the extraordinary nature of their practical intelligence. Indeed it sometimes happens that individuals who have gained distinction in a lower position carry that distinction with them to a higher position without actually earning it there. If their work is then not terribly demanding, they do not run the risk of showing any weakness. Judgment cannot distinguish very clearly what sort of reputation these people deserve, and such individuals often cause us to form a lower opinion of a personality that might, in fact, be brilliant in certain positions.

Thus distinguished service in war calls for a peculiar genius, from the lowest ranks on up. Yet history and the judgment of subsequent generations associate the name *genius* only with the minds that have excelled in the highest ranks, that is, among the commanders in chief. The reason is that the demands for intelligence and moral power are far greater at that level. (H&P 111; H 249–250)

A commander's personal characteristics are all specific and individual, but we should not refrain from making one general observation—that the most cautious and conservative individuals should not be placed at the head of subordinate armies, as is the usual practice, but rather the most *enterprising*. This brings us back to a previous point: Nothing is as important in a concerted strategic operation as that every part do its job to the fullest, to actualize the full effectiveness of its powers. In this way, deficiencies in one place can be offset by accomplishments elsewhere. We can be certain that each of the parts will give its utmost only if its leaders are quick, enterprising individuals—individuals with inner drive who throw their heart into the effort. A purely objective, cold assessment of the necessary activity rarely suffices. (H&P 632; H 1032–1033)

Hot-blooded, easily roused feelings are ill suited for everyday life, and thus also for war. They do have the merit of engendering strong impulses, but those impulses do not last. However, if the liveliness of these men takes the direction of courage and ambition, it is often quite useful in war among the lower positions of command, for the simple reason that the military action that is overseen by individuals in the lower ranks is quite short-lived. Here one bold decision, one surge of the soul's forces, is often enough. A daring attack, a rousing assault, is the work of a few minutes; an intrepid battle is the work of an entire day; and a campaign is the work of a year. (H&P 106–107; H 242–243)

The general cannot expect his corps commanders always to demonstrate the instincts, good will, courage, and character he may desire. Therefore, he cannot leave everything to their judgment but must lay out instructions on many things. Those instructions will control how they handle issues, and can easily ignore the specific circumstances of a particular case. That is unfortunate but unavoidable. If the general does not display a firm, commanding attitude that extends to each member of the body, the army cannot be properly managed. And a person who believes the best of people and expects them to make good is entirely unfit to lead an army properly. (H&P 510; H 848)

THE DIVIDENDS OF METHOD

Methods can, however, play a role in the theory of warfare, when conceived as a general way of carrying out duties whenever those duties are required (and based on average probability) or when conceived as a mastery of principles and rules all the way through to their application. They should not, however, be taken for something they are not, that is, as absolute and necessary constructs for action (systems). Instead, they should be considered the best kind of abstract forms, serving as a shortcut for individual decisions, if so desired.

We must also recognize that methodical procedure has its own positive side. The drill of constantly repetitive formulations instills *skill, precision,* and *sureness* in the leadership of troops, which reduces natural friction and makes the machine run more smoothly.

Method will be more widely used and will be more indispensable when the center of activity is further down in the ranks; the higher the rank, the less important it becomes, until it loses its attraction altogether at the highest position. For this reason, it is more suited to tactics than to strategy.

In its highest forms, war is not an *infinite number of small events* that are comparable despite their differences and that would be controlled more or less well by means of a better or worse method. Rather, it comprises *single, significant,* and *decisive* events that need to be handled individually. We are not dealing with a field of grass, which a scythe can cut down well or badly without concern for the shape of each grass blade. Instead, war is like a group of large trees: The axe must take into account each trunk's shape and direction of growth. (H&P 153; H 308–309)

THE SUM OF THE INDIVIDUAL VICTORIES

As we have said elsewhere, each type of terrain and ground, as it approaches the extreme, has the effect of weakening the supreme commander's influence on the outcome in equal proportion to the increases in the strength of his subordinates, right down to the common soldier. The more the forces are divided, the more impossible it is to oversee them, and the more each person acting in war is left to his own devices. That is obvious. Of course, as the action becomes increasingly divided, diversified, and varied, the more the influence of the intelligence must increase in general. Even the commander in chief will be able to demonstrate greater understanding in that situation.

But we must repeat what we have already said, namely, that in war, the sum of the individual outcomes is more important than the manner in which they are connected. Therefore, if we carry this viewpoint to the extreme, and think of the army as being extended in a long firing line in which each soldier fights his own little battle, it is the sum of the individual victories that matters more than the manner in which they are connected. This is because the effectiveness of good combinations can derive only from positive results, not from negative ones. So the courage, skill, and spirit of the individual is the most important thing in this case. Only when armies are of equal merit, or when the particular qualities of each are equally balanced, can the talent and insight of the commander once again be a decisive factor. (H&P 349–350; H 604–605)

The Moral Virtues
of the Commander

HONOR

O f all the intense feelings that swell the human heart in the
thick of the battle, we must honestly confess that none is
as powerful and unwavering as the soul's thirst for honor
and glory, which the German language deals with so unjustly. The
language attempts to disparage them through two reprehensible
notions in the words *Ehrgeiz* (desire for honor) and *Ruhmsucht*
(craving for fame). Of course, the abuse of this noble ambition has
been the cause of the most outrageous injustices against humanity
in war, but, in consideration of their origins, these emotions must
be counted among the most honorable of which man is capable. In
war, they are the very breath of life that stirs the vast undertaking.
All other emotions, no matter how much more common they may
be, or how much higher they may appear to be—patriotism, ideal-
ism, revenge, enthusiasm of any kind—do not make the desire for
honor and fame any less necessary. Those emotions may well stir
the masses to general action, and may inspire them, but they do not

give a commander the yearning to accomplish more than his com-
panions, a vital aspect of his position if he is to do great things.
Unlike the desire for honor, they cannot turn individual military
acts, as it were, into the personal possessions of the leader, which he
then strives to use to best advantage, plowing strenuously, sowing
carefully in hopes of a rich harvest. Yet it is these very efforts of all
leaders, from the highest to the lowest level, this industriousness,
this competitiveness, this stimulus, that gives life to an army's
actions, and makes it successful. As for what concerns the commander in chief, we must ask: Has there ever been a great commander who was not filled with ambition, or is such a person even
conceivable? (H&P 105; H 239–240)

BOLDNESS

We believe, then, that it is impossible to imagine a distinguished
commander who is lacking in boldness. In other words, someone
not born with this strength of character cannot become such a
commander; boldness, then, is the first requirement for such a
career. The second issue is how much of this innate strength, which
is expanded and modified through education and life's experiences,
the individual retains by the time he reaches a senior position. The
more this quality remains, the stronger beat the wings of genius—
and the higher it soars. The risk is all the greater, but so is the goal.
Whether actions originate in and are guided by some remote necessity or are, rather, the keystone to some ambitious scheme, or
whether the actions are those of a Frederick or an Alexander, is all
more or less the same from the standpoint of criticism. If the latter
intrigues the imagination more because it is more daring, the former is more pleasing to the intellect, because its inner necessity is
greater. (H&P 192; H 369–370)

Let us concede that in war, boldness has its own privileges.
Beyond the success of calculations concerning space, time, and the

Honor

William Shakespeare gave dramatic expression to the value of honor to both the commander and the fighting man. This speech by King Henry V has become one of the best known appeals—real or fictitious—to defend country and honor.

William Shakespeare — *Henry V;* act III, scene I

Once more into the breach, dear friends, once more;
Or close the wall up with our English dead!
In peace there's nothing so becomes a man
As modest stillness and humility:
But when the blast of war blows in our ears,
Then imitate the action of the tiger;
Stiffen the sinews, summon up the blood,
Disguise fair nature with hard-favour'd rage;
Then lend the eye a terrible aspect;
Let it pry through the portage of the head
Like the brass cannon; lew the brow o'erwhelm it
As fearfully as doth a galled rock
O'erhang and jutty his confounded base,
Swill'd with the wild and wasteful ocean.
Now set the teeth and stretch the nostril wide,
Hold hard the breath, and bend up every spirit
To his full height! On, on, you noblest English,
Whose blood is fet from fathers of war-proof!
Fathers that, like so many Alexanders,
Have in these parts from morn till even fought,
And sheath'd their swords for lack of argument.
Dishonour not your mothers; now attest
That those whom you call'd fathers did beget you!
Be copy now to men of grosser blood,

> And teach them how to war. And you, good yeoman,
> Whose limbs were made in England, show us here
> The mettle of your pasture. Let us swear
> That you are worth your breeding; which I doubt not,
> For there is none of you so mean and base
> That hath not noble luster in your eyes.
> I see you stand like greyhounds in the slips,
> Straining upon the start. The game's afoot!
> Follow your spirit; and, upon this charge
> Cry "God for Harry! England and Saint George!"

size of forces, boldness must be granted a certain entitlement that it gains when it proves its superiority, drawing that entitlement from the weakness of its opponent. It is, therefore, a truly creative force. (H&P 190; H 366)

The further we go up the chain of command, the more necessary it becomes for boldness to go hand in hand with a superior mind so that it does not become pointless, the prodding of blind passion. The issue becomes far less one of self-sacrifice and much more one of protecting others and the well-being of the whole. Therefore, deliberation must govern in the commander, whereas ingrained service regulations govern in the masses of soldiers. Boldness in a particular action may easily prove to be a mistake, but this shortcoming is worthwhile, one that cannot be regarded in the same way as other mistakes. Happy the army where inopportune boldness is commonplace; it is a lush and wild plant, but one that gives evidence of a rich soil. Even recklessness, that is, boldness without any purpose, is not something to be disdained. Basically, it is the same character trait, but one exercised in the heat of passion, without any thought involved. Only when boldness revolts against the mind's obedience, where it disregards an express command, must it be dealt with as a dangerous evil, not for its own sake, but because of the failure to obey a command, for in war, obedience is supreme. (H&P 190–191; H 367)

Lucid thought and mental control rob feelings of most of their power. That is why boldness *becomes less common the further up in rank we go.* Although discernment and understanding may not increase with rank, objective realities, conditions, and considerations will affect the commanders in their various posts often and to a profound degree; *these factors will weigh all the more heavily on commanders the less they really understand them.* In war, this is the main reason for the experience expressed in the French proverb: "Tel brille au second qui s'éclipse au premier" [A man who shines at the second level may be eclipsed at the first level]. Nearly all the generals familiar to us from history as second-rate or even irresolute had distinguished themselves in lower ranks by their boldness and determination. (H&P 191; H 367–368)

Although strategy is the exclusive territory of generals or senior commanders, boldness in the rest of the army is still at least equally important to strategy as any other military virtue. With an army drawn from a bold people, in which the spirit of boldness has always been nurtured, more can be done than with a people to whom this military virtue is unknown. That is why we have discussed boldness with respect to the army, although our actual subject is the boldness of the commander.

The further up we go in the command structure, the more the mind, the intellect, and understanding prevail, and consequently the more boldness, which is a quality of the temperament, is suppressed. This is why boldness is so rare in the upper ranks, but all the more marvelous when it is found there. Boldness guided by superior intellect is the mark of a hero. This boldness does not consist in fighting against the nature of things, in blatant violation of the law of probability; rather, it consists in powerfully supporting the higher calculations through which the rhythm of the intellect races, half unaware, in making lightning-fast decisions. As boldness lends a stronger wing to the mind and insight, the higher they will soar and the farther they will see, leading to ever greater results. (H&P 191–192; H 368–369)

PERSEVERANCE

In war, more than anywhere else in the world, things turn out differently from what we expected, and look differently up close from how they looked at a distance. How calmly the architect can watch his work rise up, seeing his drawings take shape! A doctor, though far more exposed to unfathomable circumstances and chance than the architect, still is familiar with the means at his disposal and knows quite accurately what effects they will have. In war, the commander of a large army finds himself in a constant swell of false and true reports; of mistakes made through fear, carelessness, or excessive haste; of disobedience to his orders resulting from correct or incorrect views, ill will, a true or false sense of duty, sluggishness, or exhaustion; and of accidents that no one could have foreseen. In short, he is the victim of a hundred thousand impressions, most of which are worrisome and few of which are encouraging.

Long experience of war affords the instinct for quickly assessing the value of these individual events; great courage and inner strength hold up under them, just as the rocks endure through the pounding of the waves. Anyone who gave in to these impressions would never complete any of his undertakings. For this reason, *perseverance* in the chosen course is a vital counterbalance, as long as there are no compelling reasons against it. Moreover, in war there is hardly any glorious undertaking that can be accomplished without an infinite amount of effort, trouble, and privation. Since human physical and mental weakness is always prepared to give up, only great strength of will that is expressed in a steadfastness that is admired by the world and by future generations can lead us to our goal. (H&P 193; H 371–372)

Only general principles and perspectives can be the result of a clear and deep understanding. They guide affairs from a *higher* standpoint and serve as an anchor for opinions about pending individual cases. But the difficulty lies in holding firmly to the fruit of earlier reflection when confronted with the opinions and appearances of the present moment. A wide gap often stands between the specific instance and the basic principle, and there is not always a clear chain of reasoning between the two. In those cases, a measure of self-confidence is required, and a certain skepticism is healthy. Often our only aid is a rule-making principle that, though removed from the realm of reflection, governs reflection itself. It is the principle that in the event of doubt, *we must keep to our original opinion and not deviate from it until a clear reason convinces us otherwise.* We must be strong in the belief that well-tested principles lead us closer to the truth, and not let the *vividness* of momentary appearances cause us to forget that they are less genuine. In moments of doubt, our preference for our former conviction endows our affairs with a consistency and continuity that people call character.

It is easy to see just how much an even temperament contributes to strength of character. Because of this, people of great fortitude usually have great character.

Having considered strength of character, we turn now to a deformation of that same trait—obstinacy. In specific instances, it is often hard to tell where one ends and the other begins. The conceptual difference, however, is not hard at all.

Obstinacy is not a *defect of the understanding.* By obstinacy, we mean an opposition to better judgment, and it would be a contradiction to attribute that to understanding, which is the power of judgment. Rather, obstinacy is a *defect of the emotions.* The unwillingness to bend, a resistance to judgments not one's own, only have their basis in a particular type of *selfishness,* which places above every other *pleasure* that of *using one's mind to exert control over oneself and others.* We would call it a form of vanity if it were not something better. Vanity is satisfied with appearances, whereas obstinacy is a pleasure that concerns the thing itself.

We can therefore say that strength of character becomes obstinacy when opposition to the judgment of others is not based on more convincing evidence or reliance on a higher principle, but on a *feeling of opposition*. Although this definition does not give us much practical help, it does at least prevent obstinacy from being considered a *mere increase* in one's strength of character. In essence, it is something quite different, though similar and related. An increase in intensity has so little to do with it that we will find highly obstinate people who, because they lack understanding, have little character. (H&P 108–109; H 245–246)

SELF-CONTROL

But we believe we are closer to the truth when we suppose that the power to submit to reason even in the throes of the strongest emotion, which we call *self-control,* is itself located in the seat of emotion. It is itself a feeling, which in people of strong character balances an excited passion without destroying it, and only an equilibrium of this type can ensure that reason remains in control. This equilibrium is nothing more than the sense of human worth, that most noble pride, that most inner need of the soul to *act in all cases as a being endowed with understanding and reason.* We would therefore say that a strong character is one that *does not lose its equilibrium when confronted with the strongest emotions.* (H&P 106; H 241)

BEYOND STRATEGY

*In which author and strategist alike
must venture one small but crucial step beyond strategy
lest the entire effort
be of not the slightest consequence whatsoever.*

One does not start a war, or one should not reasonably do so, without first determining what one intends to accomplish through the war, and in it. The first is the war's ultimate purpose, the second its intermediate objective. This overriding thought sets the course, determines the scope of the means used and the amount of effort, having a profound influence right down to the smallest details of the operation. (H&P 579; H 952)

War is no pastime, not merely a desire for daring and winning, not an undertaking for unbridled enthusiasm. It is a serious means to a serious end. Everything about it that is reminiscent of a colorful game of chance, everything that it possesses of the wild swings of passion, courage, imagination, and enthusiasm, are merely characteristics of this means.

War between communities—between entire peoples, and particularly *civilized* peoples—always stems from a political condition, and is brought about solely on the basis of a policy motive. It is, therefore, a political act. If war were a complete, uninterrupted, and absolute expression of violence, as we would have to conclude from the pure concept, from the very instant that it is brought about through policy, it would replace policy as something quite independent from it; war would take the place of policy and follow its own laws alone, just as a mine, when it explodes, can no longer be directed and guided in any other way than as it was previously set. This is how the situation has been thought of so far, even in practice, whenever some lack of accord between policy and the conduct of war has led to such theoretical distinctions.

Yet this is not how things are, and this view is utterly wrong. As we have seen, war in the real world is not such an extreme event that discharges its tension in a single blow. Rather, it is the effect of forces that do not develop entirely in the same way and evenly, but that rise up sufficiently, at one point, to overcome the resistance that inertia and friction create, but on another occasion are too weak to have any impact at all. So war is, in a manner of speaking, a pulsa-

Of Goals and Sovereign Purpose

Among the many philosophical contributions of Clausewitz, none has been as influential both within and outside the realm of military affairs as his distinction between goals and purpose, and the subordination of military activity to the political will of a nation that is derived from this distinction. Purpose, according to Clausewitz, is the superior intelligence, the guiding principle, the political reason that leads a nation, the sovereign, to engage in war. Military goals, the objectives of campaigns, exist merely to serve the sovereign purpose; hence his famous maxim that war is a "continuation of policy by other means." This statement has often been fatally misinterpreted to mean that war should be considered as simply one of many options for realizing political objectives and hence that war is business as usual. It is true—although hard to realize for us now—that Clausewitz, as almost all thinkers since antiquity until very recently, considered war a natural and indeed necessary element of the human condition. It is utterly wrong, however, to suggest that Clausewitz would have considered war merely a political tool to be used as freely and opportunistically as other tools.

Although a military man to his bones who chafed under the pleasantries of civilian life, Clausewitz's own enormous strength of character is evident in breaking with the strong militaristic tendencies of his times by unequivocally demanding that all aspects of the military be always considered part of and subservient to the greater purpose of the sovereign.

The corollary distinction between goals in strategy and a larger sovereign purpose may not yet have attained the significance that it deserves in business. Are, for example, growth and gain in market share typical strategic goals, and profitability and shareholders' value the sole sovereign purpose? In recent years some companies and a few business thinkers have started to question this facile interpretation and to express their intuition of something larger and more encompassing. Over the last few decades the influence of business on almost all aspects of social institutions and life has attained a previously unimaginable breadth and depth. Whereas in the

recent past and ever before business was merely an appendix to society—
albeit a very useful one—and not held in high esteem, in recent years it has
occupied the central stage of society. Whether this is to be condemned as a
growing number of critics would have it, or to be delighted in as some business leaders and policymakers do, must remain unresolved here, but the
fact is undeniable. And if one does accept the fact, one cannot fail to see
that the distinction between goals and sovereign purpose in business has
now acquired a meaning that it lacked in the past.

Having suffused deeply and inextricably into the fabric and indeed
the very fibers of society, businesses can no longer afford to simply view
society as a collection of markets, consumers, and employees whose economic needs can be profitably satisfied; they must accept their larger and
far more responsible roles in contributing to the health, not merely the
prosperity, of society.

tion of greater or lesser violence, thus discharging its tensions and
exhausting its forces more or less slowly. In other words, war leads
to its goal more or less quickly, but always lasts long enough to exert
influence on the goal in the process so that it may take one direction or another—in short, remain subject to the will of a guiding
intelligence. When we consider that war proceeds from a political
purpose, it is quite natural that this first motive, which brought
forth the war, also remains the most important consideration in
directing it. Yet this does not make the political purpose into a sort
of despotic lawgiver. It must adapt itself to the nature of the means
at hand, and is often changed in so doing; but it must still be what is
taken into consideration first. Policy, therefore, permeates all military action and exerts a continual influence on it, to the extent that
the nature of the forces exploding within it allows. (H&P 86–87;
H 209–210)

We see, then, that war is not merely a political act, but truly a
political instrument, a continuation of political will carried out by

other means. What still remains peculiar to war relates solely to the particular nature of its means. The art of war in general and the commander in each individual instance can insist that the directions and intentions of policy not conflict with these means. This demand is no small matter. Yet no matter how heavily its influence may be felt on the political designs in individual instances, it must still be regarded merely as a modification of them, for the political purposes are the ends, and war is the means. The means can never be considered separately from the ends. (H&P 87; H 210)

★ ★ ★ ★

What we previously said about the war plan in general, and about the destruction of the opponent in particular, was intended to place the war plan's goal above all else. We then sought to lay out the basic principles that should guide us in determining the ways and means. In doing so, we hoped to see clearly what is done and should be done in such a war. We wanted to emphasize the necessary and general while giving the individual and accidental their due. But we tried to distance ourselves from what is *arbitrary, unfounded, trivial, fanciful,* or *sophistic.* If we have achieved this goal, we consider our task complete. (H&P 632–633; H 1033)

Clausewitz on Clausewitz

It is not *what* we have thought, but rather *how* we have thought it, that we consider to be our contribution to theory.

Sources for Sidebars

"Love in the Life of Clausewitz," p. 8. Wilhelm von Schramm, *Clausewitz. Leben und Werk,* 3rd ed. (Esslingen: Bechtle Verlag, 1981).

"The Hardships and Rewards of Reading Clausewitz," p. 10. Prussian "Militär-Literatur-Zeitung" from 1832 as quoted by Werner Hahlweg, "Das Clausewitzbild einst und jetzt," *Vom Kriege: Hinterlassenes Werk des Generals Carl von Clausewitz,* 19th ed. (Bonn: Ferdinand Dümmlers Verlag, 1991).

"Penetrating Uncertainty," p. 55. Daniel J. Hughes, ed., *"On Strategy"* (1871), *Count Helmuth von Moltke: On the Art of War— Selected Writings* (Novato, CA: Presidio, 1993), pp. 45–46.

"Clausewitz on Scharnhorst," p. 57. Von Schramm, *Clausewitz,* p. 434f.

"F. Scott Fitzgerald on Opposed Ideas," p. 60. F. Scott Fitzgerald, *The Crack-Up,* ed. Edmund Wilson (Norfolk, CT: New Directions, 1945), pp. 70–71.

"Indeterminacy and Freedom," p. 65. Leo Tolstoy, *War and Peace,* trans. Constance Garnett (Modern Library, 1994).

"Deferral of Closure," p. 67. Susanne K. Langer, *Mind: An Essay on Human Feeling,* vol. I (Baltimore: The Johns Hopkins University Press, 1975), p. 17.

"Slide-Rule Theorists Then and Now," p. 69. Tolstoy, *War and Peace.*

"Rationalism and Romanticism in *On War*," p. 78. Michael I. Handel, ed., *Introduction to Clausewitz and Modern Strategy* (London: Frank Cass, 1986), p. 6.

"Strife and Origination," p. 82. René Thom, *Structural Stability and Morphogenesis: An Outline of a General Theory of Models* (Reading, MA: Addison-Wesley, 1994), p. 323.

"Knightean Uncertainty," p. 90. Handel, *Introduction to Clausewitz,* p. 14.

"Friction and Learning," p. 94. Clayton M. Christensen, *The Innovator's Dilemma: When New Technologies Cause Great Firms to Fail* (Boston: Harvard Business School Press, 1997), pp. 160–161.

"A Freely Creative Activity," p. 101. Ludwig Beck, *Studien,* ed. Hans Speidel (Stuttgart: K.F. Koehler Verlag, 1955), pp. 130–131.

"Lessons from Military Strategy," p. 117. Bruce Henderson, *The Logic of Business Strategy* (Cambridge, MA: Ballinger, 1984), pp. 4–5.

"Remaking the Rules," p. 138. Carlos Fuentes, *The Old Gringo* (New York: Noonday Press, Farrar Straus Giroux, 1997), pp. 77, 82.

"Moltke on Chance and Luck," p. 142. Hughes, "*On Strategy*" (1871), *Count Helmuth von Moltke,* pp. 45–46.

"Borodino," p. 147. Tolstoy, *War and Peace.*

"Honor," p. 175. William Shakespeare, *Henry V*, ed. George Lyman
Kittredge, rev. Irving Ribner (Waltham, MA: Blaisdell Publishing, 1967).

"Clausewitz on Clausewitz," p. 185. *Clausewitz, Hinterlassene Werke
über Krieg und Kriegführung*, vol. 7 (Berlin, 1862), p. 311, quoted
according to Petra Ahrweiler, "Clausewitz als Repräsentant des
wissenschaftlichen Weltverhältnisses der beginnenden Moderne," in *Clausewitz-Kolloquium. Theorie des Krieges als Sozialwis-
senschaft*, ed. Gerhard Vowinckel, Beiträge zur Politischen
Wissenschaft, vol. 65 (Berlin: Duncker & Humblot, 1993), pp.
97–110, p. 97.

Index